ⅬINCOLN CH W9-CCW-334

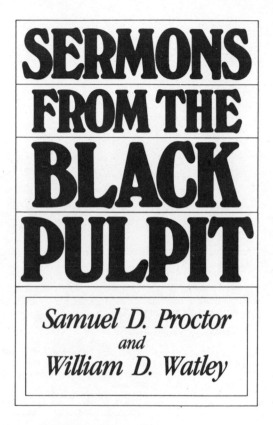

SERMONS FROM THE BLACK PULPIT

Samuel D. Proctor
and
William D. Watley

Judson Press® Valley Forge

SERMONS FROM THE BLACK PULPIT
Copyright © 1984
Judson Press, Valley Forge, PA 19482-0851

All rights reserved. No part of this publication may be reproduced, stored in a retrieval system, or transmitted in any form or by any means, electronic, mechanical, photocopying, recording, or otherwise, without the prior permission of the copyright owner, except for brief quotations included in a review of the book.

Bible quotations in this volume are from *The Holy Bible,* King James Version.

Library of Congress Cataloging in Publication Data

Proctor, Samuel D.
  Sermons from the black pulpit.
  1. Sermons, American—Afro-American authors.
I. Watley, William D. II. Title.
BV4241.5.P76 1984   252'.061   83-26744
ISBN 0-8170-1034-3

The name JUDSON PRESS is registered as a trademark in the U.S. Patent Office. Printed in the U.S.A. ⊕

Bookstore

4 77

86 nou 7

10 nou

Acknowledgments

I could never begin to thank everyone who led me to the ideas expressed in these sermons. I am deeply indebted to a wide circle of friends, family, teachers, and counselors for their help and encouragement that have brought me to the ideas expressed in the pages that follow. I shall never be able, adequately, to show my gratitude for the influence of my grandmother, Hattie Ann Fisher Proctor, for the inspiration and discipline that she introduced to me as a boy; my appreciation for loving and caring parents, Herbert and Velma, and my devoted sister and brothers throughout my lifetime; for the Sunday school teachers, members and pastors of the Bank Street Baptist Church of Norfolk, Virginia, the seminal ground for all that I cherish most; for Dr. John M. Ellison and all of those faithful ministers, college and seminary professors who opened my mind to ever-widening vistas of learning and service; for the congregations of the Pond Street Baptist Church of Providence, Rhode Island, where I began my ministry, and the Abyssinian Baptist Church of New York City, where I presently serve, for their nurture and loyalty; and for my wife Bessie Tate Proctor and our four sons, Herbert, Timothy, Sam-

73926

uel, and Steven, who have been my steady and unfailing partners in every endeavor. For their patience and care in performing secretarial assistance through the tedious assignments laid upon them, I wish to thank Esther McCall, Elizabeth Smallwood, and Lorraine Smoller.

Samuel D. Proctor

There are four persons that I would like to recognize:

First, my parents, Rev. and Mrs. Matthew A. Watley, who have set an example of sound preaching, right practice, and effective ministry. These sermons are dedicated to them and their ministry.

Second, my wife Muriel, not only for her patience and understanding during the refining process for the sermons in this book, but also for her love and faithfulness, her support and encouragement during these years that I have endeavored to be a proclaimer of the Word/word.

Third, Mrs. Carolyn Scavella, beloved sister and friend, for invaluable editorial and typing assistance.

William D. Watley

Introduction

Drawing from events and personalities of the Old and New Testaments, the authors provide sermons that will nourish the preacher. These sermons creatively lift up what it means to live the abundant life as a people of God. The best of biblical scholarship and theological reflection are evidenced in affirming what it means to be a person under God. The Scripture is interpreted clearly and concisely. The illustrations from life are penetrating. In a relevant sermonic style the authors are intentional in expressing the cultural, social, political, economic, as well as religious realities of our world as they are and as they ought to be.

The preacher needs to be nourished and sustained. The community and congregation expect the preacher to be prophetic, priestly, programmatic, diplomatic, dramatic, and compassionate. With so many roles and expectations tugging at the person of the preacher, these sermons are a usable resource for assisting the preacher in preparing for the preaching event.

Contents

The Recovery of Human Compassion

Samuel D. Proctor

Luke 10:25-37

This title implies that we once knew what compassion is or that we were never perfectly a compassionate people. Nevertheless, we're now seeing one of the worst contradictions in our nation's history, a nation that boasts of having a society that rests upon the Judeo-Christian values.

What is this contradiction? Loud noises are being made in the name of Christ, but these noises are often made by persons who are not at all enthusiastic about what we understand to be the compassion of our Lord. "Compassion" means "to suffer with."

The theme of compassion runs through all that Jesus said and did. The way in which he seemed to feel the very pulse of an epileptic child's heartbeat, the way in which he sensed the tension and strain of a woman who had to touch his garment, the way in which he could *suffer with* the hurt and the pain and the sorrow and the loneliness of those whom he had not even known very long, all of these point to his compassion. The lasting and fundamental impression that Jesus makes on the mind is his compassion, his empathy, and his sympathy for other persons.

9

Some years ago, I was with a group that went out under the sponsorship of the Baptist World Alliance, preaching in Eastern Europe, in Russia, and even in Latvia. We had a wonderful time. We even had a chance to preach in that great downtown Baptist Church in Moscow. But when we were there, we were not allowed to move about freely.

We had a tour guide who followed us everywhere. And because we traveled by car over much of the territory, we had a chance to talk extensively with her in private. We found out that she knew hardly anything at all about Jesus and had great contempt for the whole subject of Christianity. We found out that her friends had not thought much at all about Christianity. They were forbidden to study it or to converse about it.

So I decided that every time I chose a text on which to preach, I would not go into a topical sermon. I would simply tell one story after another about Jesus and his encounters with people (for our guide's benefit mostly), and I would tell them all in great detail. I would not hasten or overlook his mood or one single inflection, and then I would end the story right there, without embellishment.

As we were leaving Moscow, I said to her, "Ilka, you've heard a lot of sermons since you've been traveling with us." She said, "Oh, yes." I asked, "What is your conclusion? You said you did not know much about Jesus at first. Now what do you think?" She said she did not want to answer that. But at the train station, when we were about to board and head for the north, into Latvia, she eased over to me and said, "You want to know what I think about Jesus? Jesus was a wonderful person!"

That's what anyone would have to conclude who studied the Gospels carefully. Nowhere is this truth any more clearly displayed than in the simple story Jesus told—and one that the world can never forget—about compassion. This is found in Luke 10 in thirteen short verses (25-37).

A crowd had gathered to listen to Jesus as he taught. A man who was a law professor, one skilled in the religious dogmas of Jesus' own tradition, a kind of "Ph.D." in rabbinical studies, stood up to ask a question. The crowd was, no doubt, stunned to silence, for it seemed that a real confrontation had begun. A crowd likes a confrontation. Jesus, the barefooted son of a carpenter, on the one side, and this rabbinical expert, with his scholar's shawl draped over his shoulder, on the other. The scholar asked, "Master, what shall I do to inherit eternal life?"

Jesus saw that the question was a snare or a trick. It was asked only to bring criticism upon him, and so Jesus did not answer directly. He let the professor answer his own question.

Jesus replied, "What does your law say? You have studied it. How do you interpret it?"

The professor answered, "Thou shalt love the Lord thy God with all thy heart, with all thy soul, with all thy strength, and with all thy mind; and thy neighbor as thyself."

Now Jesus knew these words all too well. They were found in the ancient law of his people. He had, no doubt, heard them as a boy in his own synagogue. And when he heard this answer from the professor, Jesus agreed with him and said, "Correct. Do just that and you will inherit eternal life."

But the professor did not want it to end there, and he pressed the point: "Who is my neighbor?" In other words, he was asking, "Who am I supposed to love? How wide is the circle of persons that I must acknowledge as my neighbor? For after all, I am a member of a very special people, and I have special standing among these special people." (This is paraphrased to make the issue clear.) When he raised that point, Jesus decided not to debate any further.

Jesus then painted one of those pictures that he often painted, a word picture. He told one of those compact stories that has a profound truth buried in every phrase. The story is only one paragraph long but it is chock-full. It's really like the overture of an opera in which all the themes of the opera are poured into one brief, resounding prelude.

He started out, "A certain man. . . ." He wouldn't give away the identity of the man's tribe, his race, his clan, his social class, his dialect, or even the language he spoke. We don't need to know any of that! Why do we need footnotes on him? Jesus left all that information out! Just *Homo sapiens*, that's all. A certain man, it could have been anybody, was simply on his way from Jerusalem to Jericho. If we ask about the man's background and all of that, we start ruining the whole story. Jesus wants to leave the subject right there.

The journey was seventeen dangerous miles through lonely, rocky, rough desert, and it is still seventeen lonely miles even today. Robbers and muggers were known to attack travelers, and this man was beaten by thieves and left half dead. In the story Jesus had the man's clothes torn off and had him unconscious so that we can not identify him by his clothes; we can't tell anything by the cut of his garment, the depth of the border, the hem of the cloth, or the color of the cloth. We can't tell whether he was a poor man with a cheaply woven piece of cloth or a rich man with a cloth of smooth purple and a deep hem. We don't have the advantage of getting our prejudices working. He was "a certain man." Jesus left him naked so we wouldn't have any clue whatsoever as to his status; and he was unconscious so we can't hear his accent. We don't know whether he said "sibboleth" or "shibboleth."

So, since he was without clothes and was unconscious, we can't tell who was lying there. Jesus was trying to fix it so that all we have to deal with is the man's suffering. Jesus removed every other detail. He was hurt! Without clothes and unconscious, there the man lay. He could have been a person of our own race and class, and we might have helped out of ethnic pride and loyalty, not out of pure compassion. He could have been one of another race and class. Jesus made the story tell of nothing but a human being in need, half dead, beaten, and robbed. We don't know how well educated he was or how poor he was. We don't know what family he came from or what side of town he lived on. Barely breathing, bloody, and near death the "certain man" was left to die.

A priest came by and saw the man and would not get near him. He crossed the street to avoid him. In those days, the dead had to be handled in a very special way, and a priest believed that he could be defiled by touching a dead body that had not been handled according to the prescribed rituals. A life was hanging in the balance, but the priest was worried about staying pure and not getting defiled by an unidentified, dying body.

"Then," Jesus said, "a Levite came by also." He was upper-middle class, well-to-do, a member of a closed fraternity, from a proper family, with the best education of the day. He did pause and look at the man, but since the man had no clothes on, how could the Levite tell who he was? And since he was unconscious the Levite could not hear his speech. He would never have taken a chance on being seen on the Jericho road with the body of a person beneath his class or status or one of another race or nation. Hung up on class and station and tribe and clan as he was, the Levite passed by on the other side, too.

Then a Samaritan came by, one of a mixed race, a despised people. He was too "unclean" from birth ever to enter the temple, one whose son could not date the professor's daughter, one who would never be invited to dinner at the Levite's apartment, and one who might have been beaten on that road himself just for being a Samaritan.

"The Samaritan was filled with compassion," said Jesus. He went straight toward the man and poured his own oil and wine on the man's wounds to keep out infection, wrapped the wounds with his own headpiece that he needed to keep the desert sand out of his nose and eyes, put the man on his own donkey, and walked slowly alongside until he reached an inn. The Samaritan stayed with the man all night, not knowing his race, his tribe, his pedigree, or the cause of his tragedy, but knowing only that he needed help. Compassion! And the next day the Samaritan told the innkeeper to let the man stay there until he got well. He paid for three weeks in advance and said, "If it costs more than that, I'll pay you when I come this way again." He was leaving his "Visa Card" with the innkeeper!

Then Jesus looked up at the law professor and said, "Tell me which of these men acted like a neighbor?" He said, "He that showed mercy." Jesus said, "You go and do the same."

This is a familiar story, but it's like some of the hymns we sing: the words are so well known that we really don't hear them. It's sort of like a siren wailing on a downtown street at night or a barking dog—both are heard but unheeded. And I suppose that this is why we need preachers to take these familiar truths, these time-worn words and stories, and lift them up and declare them in the language of this day. We need to amplify them and let their messages find us where we are in our own time and in our own world. We need them, in our own idiom, right now.

This compassion that Jesus talked about must not be regarded as something for naive and simple-minded people. We often use the label "Christian" to give a respectable designation for our schemes and predilections, but they do not necessarily bear the marks of the compassion of Christ. We march under this Christian flag, and we chant these Christian melodies and we celebrate these Christian festivals. But our culture is ruthless—it leaves homeless people sleeping in train stations. It is violent—it allows death-dealing drugs to exploit and destroy the poor. It is cold—it treats children as though they asked to be born in tough ghettos. It is uncaring—it penalizes the indigent aged for growing old and getting sick. It is lacking in compassion, and we are *supposed* to be the salt of the earth and the leaven in the lump. We are to be the remnant, now, to save *our* culture from this cold and violent and uncompassionate way of life.

We have come to recognize the lack of compassion of our cities, our government, our communities, our institutions, and we find that they are all passing by on the other side. The world has become a heartless place. We've gotten so used to it that we're practically numb to the inhumanity, to the callous indifference that surrounds us.

In my home state of New Jersey, we face budget shortages, just as every other state does, running out of money for education and social services especially. And without any great controversy whatsoever, we installed gambling casinos in Atlantic City. When you go down there—if you thought this was not a social problem at first—see who's down there gambling: old folk with their Social Security payments, poor folk, women without husbands and who live alone, and people with the familiar signs of insecurity. There they are, taking this last chance at trying to augment their livelihood. We would rather take from the poor like that than raise the money in other ways and take care of the needs of our state. I have seen Brink's trucks all of my life hauling money, but I had never seen a fourteen-wheel rig with "Brink's" printed on its side until I saw one coming out of Atlantic City one night. A truckload of poor folks' money! Our state has a budget that counts on several million dollars a year coming out of Atlantic City. That says nothing of what will filter out of Miami Beach and out of Las Vegas. We do this with casual ease: we walk by on the other side.

Here we are, rid of smallpox and yellow fever. We're finished with poliomyelitis and tuberculosis. We're able to reconnect severed limbs and to reproduce skin tissues, ready now to create cancer cells and produce their antibodies. We expect to find a vaccine for almost everything that bothers us, even some kind of vaccine from deoxyribonucleic acid research for mental diseases. But we cannot change the moral climate of our culture.

We cannot change the hearts of persons. We cannot create a caring spirit among us.

We haven't found out how to educate people in compassion. We are educating more people than ever before. More degrees are granted than the world has ever seen, but we are a nation of violent, unloving strangers still with more casual, but painful, divorces, more child abuse, more husband and wife abuse, and with suicide rampant. With all of our technological achievements and major advancements in medicine, here we are no better off morally and spiritually than those people a long time ago who first heard Jesus tell about a man who fell among thieves on the Jericho road. We need to recover a sense of human compassion.

One day in January, upon arriving in Chicago's O'Hare Airport, I saw an account in the morning paper (how does this sound for a civilized society?): A twenty-two-year-old woman and her twenty-six-year-old boyfriend found a blind man standing alone in a snowstorm just before dark, waiting for a bus. He had been to the eye clinic at the Martha Washington Hospital, and he could not find the bus stop exactly because the snow had fallen in sheets and had hidden his landmarks. While he was feeling in the snow frantically for something he could recognize, they spotted him. They drove close by. The couple said, "Blind man, we'll give you a ride if you want one. You're not going to find your way home." He agreed and they took him in their car. But instead of giving the blind man a ride home, they stopped in the freezing weather at the waterfront on Lake Michigan, right on the lake where the winter wind feels like it's separating flesh from bones. There they pretended to have car trouble and asked the blind man to hold up the hood of their car while they worked under it. While he was doing that, they told him that they had a razor at his neck and took from him $15 in cash, a $340 welfare check, and a tape recorder that he used to keep notes and instructions and that sort of thing. Since he couldn't read, he used a small pocket radio for the news; he had a pocket braille calculator that he used to follow transactions and he had some credit cards. They took all of the above. And do you know they took the blind man's walking cane from him also! They left him standing there, knee-deep in the snow, with the January wind off the lake wrapping around him in the dark, alone. I have heard of a lot of things, but that was the very bottom. We know how low human nature can sink when we read of behavior like that.

At the other end of the scale is the compassion of Jesus creating a polarity to our worst impulses, tugging, pleading, persuading, empowering, and straining to break our stubborn inertia. Oh, what a privilege it is for Christian preachers to make the gospel plain, to take on a task like this and to try to get the aroma of the gospel spread throughout the land. We as a nation are in deep trouble. We're in trouble in the streets, in Congress, in corporate board rooms, in state houses, and in the White House. It all points to a crisis in our values. We need not all believe the same thing about what to do at every moment, but we must work toward some kind of consensus, and we must work hard and work together. And there is no better place to begin than on the Jericho road with this compassionate Samaritan.

As we look more closely, we observe that when Jesus told the story of the man left to die, he did not deal with *who* it was who beat him, *how* he got robbed, *why* he was on that dangerous road alone, or *whether* he had any warning or had been beaten up before. Jesus didn't go into any of that at all. Probably this was the problem of the priest who would not go near him, "I don't know anything about him. Why is he there?" Jesus simply pointed to him and said, "There he is, and what will you do about him? Are you going to leave him there, let him die, analyze his case, appoint a committee, call a meeting, arrange a research topic, or bend down and help?"

Everybody knows that all suffering has *some* cause and every condition has *some* antecedent. And, indeed we should be about looking for causes and reasons. That's what schools of social work, graduate schools, and seminaries are all about. But existentially, moment by moment, we cannot become preoccupied with analysis. We have to move with compassion, which is another whole way of thinking altogether. One way to delay, to defer, to avoid, to escape, to circumvent being compassionate is to hide the suffering in a computer somewhere, to lose it in historical backtracking, to make it obscure somehow. Perhaps that lack of information is what enabled the priest to pass by on the other side.

The issue of compassion has to do, not with how much information we have about suffering—we're drowning in information—but with how much we care about persons in their present situations. At the bottom line is loneliness, hunger, unemployment, bitterness, pain, and hurting. Yet we've grown too stonyhearted to care, and we need to recover human compassion

Now we who work in religion and theology understand clearly that the spontaneous goodness that underlies compassion cannot come from a cold and unrepentant heart. It does not flow from arrogant pride. It is the fruit of the Spirit. Somehow one must have a transformation of his or her life in order to outlive that atavistic drag on human nature, that primordial drive for survival, that original sin that comes from humankind's earliest experiment with defiance of God. We're sinners, alienated strangers, and sojourners. And our spirits will find no home until they rest with God.

So, without this spiritual rebirth, the first impulse in the face of suffering is to declare that everyone deserves what he or she has and to exempt ourselves entirely: That "certain man" had no business out there! We reason, *Didn't he know about the muggings and robbings on the Jericho road?* With that kind of thinking, there is no need for compassion. Everything is traceable. But you and I know that everyone does *not* deserve everything that has been poured into a single lifetime. I don't deserve what I have, and you don't deserve what you have, the good or the bad.

One Sunday morning I was preaching in Princeton's chapel and the daughter of Congressman H. Richardson Preyer from Greensboro, North Carolina, was reading the Scriptures. She had told me before that her daddy knew I was speaking and that he sent his regards to me. I had lived in Greensboro and had known Judge Preyer when I was at A & T State University. And as I climbed those narrow, steep steps to that high pulpit, perched out over the people, in the Princeton chapel, I was scared nearly out of my mind. On my way up those steps, the devil said to me, "Sam, now you know you have no business preaching here. You were a little shoeshine boy from Norfolk, standing out there on Monticello Avenue at Lee's Barber Shop, saying, 'Shine 'em up, five cents.'" I heard it all like a tape recording. "What are you doing up here in front of these people, with greetings from one so highly placed as Judge H. Richardson Preyer?"

Then I thought that, under normal circumstances, I *ought not* to be there! With the poverty, the racism, the ugliness, and the violence that surrounded my youth, I should have been in jail somewhere! Or I should have been drinking wine in a hallway in Harlem, or talking to myself in the street, directing traffic all doped up. The straight line from my boyhood should have ended anywhere but preaching in Princeton's chapel.

But by the grace of God, Sparks White Melton, a white Southern Baptist preacher, had heard that I was looking for a seminary to attend and that I had no money. He talked all the time with the janitor at his church about the black community. This janitor knew me, and he told Dr. Melton one day, "When you go to Ames and Brownley's Department Store to give your Bible class at the Tea Room again, the boy I'm talking about runs the elevator on the end."

One day I was standing in front of my elevator saying, "Going up?" One of the porters, who claimed that he didn't like preachers and who teased me about the ministry, walked by and said to me, "Oh, Reverend, go the hell on up! Nobody wants to go up with you." But he didn't see Dr. Melton standing right by him. Dr. Melton asked me, "What did he say to you?" I said, "Oh, he was just teasing, Dr. Melton. He didn't mean anything." He then asked, "Are you a preacher?" I said, "I'm trying to be." He came on the elevator and said, "Where are you going to school?" I said, "I don't know. I have no money. I'm afraid to apply." He said, "I'm a trustee of a mighty fine school, Crozer Seminary." And I began to tremble all over. Why should this man be bothered with me?

By the time we came to the sixth floor, he had me stop my elevator and prop the door open. He said, "I want you to write this down," and I wrote down the name of the man to whom I should write in order to find out all about Crozer. Then he arranged for me to get a scholarship through the seminary. Later I received a fellowship from Crozer to go to Yale for graduate study. All of this happened because a southern white man, in Norfolk, Virginia, in 1941, when blacks and whites didn't talk *ever* with one another like that, made a big leap across that high, mean, social barrier, moved right on above it, touched my life, and changed everything for me.

Indeed, my antecedents had not pointed to the Princeton chapel. The computers would never have punched out the result from the baseline input. Something happened that I had nothing to do with whatsoever. I did not deserve it! It was God's grace.

Some of us are not on the Jericho road today but not because of our own smarts. The man who fell among thieves need not have deserved it! Jesus did not deal with that issue. Praise God! He dealt with the man's sufferings. He said a certain man was beaten and robbed, and left to die. We cannot exempt ourselves with smug self-righteousness. If we all had to earn our well-being, where would we be? Compassion means to enter into the suffering of another where it hurts. Right now. Right here.

Look even closer and see that the Levite also passed by that dying man. The Levite was a privileged person, bound to his class and status. We all have to be very careful about this because we run the high risk of being more loyal to class and status than we are to Christ. And too much of our religion does not help us at all. It skips over his marvelous compassion.

I have an old Gideon Bible that I walked out of a hotel with one day when I was about to preach and had no Bible. I "liberated" that Bible. I'm amazed at the suggested readings on the first page, the very first page! The first New Testament reading is Matthew 1:18-23, the birth of Christ. The second is Luke 19:28, the triumphal entry into Jerusalem. The list skips *over* three years of preaching and healing and teaching and showing *compassion*. It does not recommend reading about four men tearing up the roof of a house to get a sick friend to Jesus. It does not recommend reading about a woman with a curved spine or a man with a son foaming at the mouth. It does not recommend reading about Nicodemus trying to find Jesus in the dark, or about the ten lepers herded together waiting for his healing touch. The suggested readings skip over all that!

President John McKay of Princeton Seminary once wrote a book that reminds me of the kind of religion that leaves us without compassion. Dr. McKay explained that during his days in Latin America, he realized that Christianity was ineffective because it leaped from Christmas with its songs and bells to Easter with its flowers and candles. It passed by the dusty roads of Galilee, Perea, and Judea completely, places where Jesus was showing compassion.

Have you seen people with religion like that? They want to

talk about the birth of Christ and the greatness of the incarnation; and after that they want to leap to the resurrection. But good religion deals with all the content in between, the revealing love of God at work in Christ. It is more than incense pots, gold crosses, big organs, long gowns, and deep sonorous voices.

God is not an aimless sentimentalist. If he made the world, then he is aware of all of its dimensions, and he is involved in it. If God created the order that surrounds us, then he holds us accountable to it. If he cared enough to bring Abraham out of Ur of the Chaldees and to find Moses on the backside of Mount Horeb; if he cared enough to reveal himself to us by shaking the pillars of the temple to call young Isaiah and then to brighten the sun on the Damascus Road to turn Saul of Tarsus around, then he means for us to care. He wants us to love him with such an undying love that his radiance in us will be reflected upon those who stand in need of our compassion.

Now, finally we must never forget that Jesus deliberately put a Samaritan in this story from among a great many candidates he might have chosen. It did not have to be a Samaritan, you know. Jesus could have chosen a Roman army captain, a Greek stoic teacher, a Jewish prophet, a nephew of Herod, or a playboy from a royal family. But he chose a Samaritan. I wonder how spontaneous this was to choose a despised member of a mixed race. He must have intended to show that race and class had nothing to do with virtue and that genes and status had nothing to do with compassion. He meant to make all of us candidates for goodness. From the humblest of circumstances one may find the highest of virtues; and that is one of the riches that the Christian community has to offer the world.

Some years ago when I was doing college work in the South, I went to eastern Carolina to Nash County to give a speech at a 4-H Club conference. In those days everything was segregated, and this was a black 4-H Club conference. In those days college heads routinely attended such conferences because we felt that rural young people benefitted from such visits. I listened carefully to the young man who spoke before I was to speak, and I was moved. He was very bright.

When he turned around, I shook his hand to congratulate him, and he blushed bashfully. But when he opened his eyes,

I saw that one eye was severely astigmatized. We call it "crossed"; his eye was severely "crossed." One eye sank right down in the corner, and it struck me forcefully. I thought to myself, *You mean that boy has a problem like that?* And my mind kept turning, and I forgot all about my little remarks.

I kept on saying, *Sam, here you are healthy and prosperous. You drove out here in a brand new car. You've got credit cards spilling out of your wallet. You're loaded down with Smithfield ham and orange juice, grits and oatmeal! Your eyes are perfect. Why don't you do something for that boy?* And I tried to say to myself, *I can't be bothered.* I tried to sneak past on the other side of the Jericho road; *I'm too busy for that detail. Somebody else will catch him.*

As I was riding back with our school public relations man, he said to me, "Your mind is blank, Sam. You're not talking to me." And I said, "Yeah, yeah, yeah, that's right." But God had just put it on me: "Sam, I'm not going to let you go. You saw that little country boy with those crossed eyes. You don't have anybody in your family with crossed eyes. What are you going to do?" I could hardly sleep that night.

Later I told the public-relations staff person that I wanted him to ride back over there and I wanted to find that boy. "What boy?" "The little boy with the crossed eyes." "Oh, come on, Sam, the boy's eyes have been crossed all of his life." I said, "No, I can't drop it like that, because I'm burdened with it." You keep on getting burdened if you try to let Christ lead your life; but the burden is light and his yoke is an easy yoke.

We went out there and we found him. (I had asked a county agricultural agent to get his name and address and the directions to his home.) We took one road and another road and another road, and deep into Nash County we found the little house. There we found all of the poverty and isolation that were so typical of the rural south at that time. When we spoke to his mother about helping him get surgery for his eye, she said, "The Lord made him like that; leave him like that." He said, "Will it hurt, Dr. Proctor?" I said, "If they do it, it's not going to hurt." "Who's going to do it?" "I don't know yet, but I know one thing; big as this world is and the way I'm burdened with this, if there's anybody around here who knows how to straighten out crossed eyes, he's my man and I'll find him." His mother finally gave a slow, qualified agreement.

When we came back to Greensboro, we didn't know what to do. I was reading a book on ethics by Waldo Beach. I knew Waldo Beach; he was a Duke University ethics professor. I went to see him.

"Brother Beach," I said, "you must know somebody in Durham who's big enough, an ophthalmologist with enough compassion, to straighten out one little black boy's crossed eyes." He said, "Sam, I go to a church where there's a father and his two sons who run an eye clinic in Durham. And they do that operation all the time. They are Christian folk. And if this thing is burdening you the way it is, then I'm going to burden them with it, too."

The next day the phone rang. Waldo Beach said to me, "Sam, the doctor and his dad and his brother said they'll do it if I get the boy to them." Compassion. I rushed back over to Nash County.

Now I know that the world still has its problems. I couldn't feed every hungry child in India. I couldn't solve the problems of women's rights. I couldn't solve the civil rights problem. But God will take you as God took me, and focus you on something, and then test you and see what you're going to do with it.

I went back over to Nash County and told the boy and his mother the good news. His mama started crying and praying. She said, "We'll have him there."

Now to make a long story short, his eyes were straightened out. Later on, he asked if I would write a reference for him to go to Livingstone College, and he made one of the finest records they ever had there. Some time after that, when I was at the University of Wisconsin, he said, "I'd like to come up there and get my Master of Business Administration degree." I got him in there, and he ripped right through that MBA. He ended up in Pittsburgh working for the Gulf Oil Company.

A little while ago, I was sitting in my office and he walked in and said, "I'm a product manager for Johnson and Johnson across the street." He said to me just before leaving, "Dr. Proctor, I want to ask you something for my own benefit. What made you take an interest in me?"

I said, "Well, I went to school a long time studying about Jesus, and I promised him over and over that I would serve him until I died. You just gave me one of the best opportunities to do just that and I seized upon it."

He asked further, "What made Dr. Beach want to do it? What made those white ophthalmologists in Durham give me a free operation like that?" "Because they're Christian folk, too. They love the Lord, too." And if you get enough folk like that, loving Jesus like that, reaching across race and clan, showing compassion, one day the kingdoms of this world *will indeed* become the kingdom of our God and of his Christ.

Everybody Is God's Somebody

Samuel D. Proctor

Acts 17:19-28

"God . . . hath made of one blood all nations . . . for to dwell on all the face of the earth . . ." (Acts 17:24-26).

Paul is now in the metropolitan center of Athens in Greece. He has left the familiar ground of Palestine, and we find him preaching in Europe, going from one big city to another. He made three preaching tours, spreading the gospel and planting new churches. The stop in Athens is on the second journey of the three. We find him here after he had answered the call from the church in Macedonia to come over and help. Here was his chance to use his training in Greek language and philosophy and to stretch out on what Gamaliel, his teacher, had drilled into him when he was a young student. He was at last preaching the gospel in Europe.

Paul, as it turned out, was really a cosmopolitan man. He was far better equipped than the disciples of Jesus—in particular Peter, James or John—to take the gospel abroad to the Hellenic centers, and now his big chance had come, for he was preaching in Athens.

Athens was the educational and cultural center of the world. Philosophers would pace up and down in the Lyceum and ponder the most profound questions about life and death, time and eternity, knowledge and feelings, the real and the illusory.

Here Socrates had taught Plato, Plato had taught Aristotle, and Aristotle had taught Alexander the Great.

To that same Athens now came a Jewish tentmaker from Tarsus, short, baldheaded, a Roman citizen, and a student of Gamaliel, preaching that Jesus Christ is the Son of God. He had come from Jerusalem and had followed the roads laid out by the engineers of the Roman army; he had preached from town to town, visiting one synagogue after another, saying, "I am not ashamed of the gospel, for it is the power of God unto salvation."

Athens was a town filled with statues, street lecturers, religious teachers, and intellectual groups; there were Stoics, Epicureans, Hedonists, and believers in all sorts of nature gods. The Athenians were accustomed to new personalities coming through, looking for followers. And Athens allowed time for these visitors to gain their own following. Nobody expected any *one* man to take the whole town. So Paul was given the same license as everyone else. They interviewed him, "What is this new doctrine you speak of?" Paul must have answered them sufficiently, for they set a date for him to have his say on Mars Hill, an open lecture area where the philosophers always spoke.

So, when his turn came, Paul moved in on them. He said that they had a town full of gods and goddesses, but he had come to tell them that there was but one God, who had made the world and all that is in it. Paul explained, "He doesn't live in temples made with hands and doesn't need any idols carved in his honor. He doesn't need anything. He has made of one blood all men to dwell on the face of the earth." Paul served notice. He did not come there to organize a small following. He came there to tell them that *the whole human race was one, that one God had made all people, and that in Christ God was bringing this whole human family to a knowledge of himself.* In other words, in Christ everybody is God's somebody.

The truth is that no matter how poorly Christians have shown it in practice, the outstanding feature of the life and teaching of Christ is that he reached beyond his own people and shed abroad the love of God in the lives of all people. Jesus treated all persons as though they were all God's children.

And the theme of Paul's sermon in Athens is this very point: God has no favorites. We are all his children, and he sent

Christ to save us all. This is what makes Christianity available to everybody. Often I hear persons glibly criticize Christianity because of the failure of individual Christians. Indeed, there may be a lot wrong with some Christians, but there's nothing wrong with Christianity. It can pass any test. There is abundant evidence that the principles of morality, ethics, and human relations that are found in Jesus' teachings meet tests of the highest scrutiny even from secular points of view; his ideas about human development are compatible with the most widely accepted ideas of modern psychology. His view of the worth of persons is the cornerstone of modern democracies.

If this world needs anything, it is a wider acceptance, a more faithful practice of, and a deeper commitment to those ideas and ideals as set forth by that marvelous preacher, teacher, and healer from Nazareth in Galilee, whom we believe to be the Son of the living God.

He not only taught these lofty concepts, but he embodied them and lived them. He stretched out his arms to the people of all nations and all backgrounds. He healed a woman's daughter of an ailment that they called "possession by the devil," and the woman was a Greek from *Syro-Phoenicia*. He healed ten lepers and one of them was from *Samaria*. He was in Capernaum one day when a *Roman* captain came and told of a servant in his house who was sick. When Jesus saw that this foreigner had faith in God, he went with him to his house to heal his servant. He was a man for *all* people. No wonder that when he was sentenced to die, the cross prepared for him was carried by a black man named Simon from *Cyrene*. No wonder that Paul's faithful helper, young Timothy, was half *Jew* and half *Greek*. Christ tore down the walls, ignored our tribal habits, and celebrated the dignity of all persons in the sight of God. In Christ everybody is God's somebody.

And Paul was only following the example of his Christ when he said, "God has made of one blood all nations. . . ." That was the theme of his great sermon on Mars Hill.

But in further witness of what Christ teaches, there is the obvious physical kinship—that all men are made of one blood. The great contribution of the black medical expert Dr. Charles Drew was his proof to the world that except for blood types — types that *all* races have in common—human blood is the same. He pioneered in taking ordinary blood from anyone and dehydrating it. He made it into squares like yeast cakes—blood from *anybody*—and on the battlefields it was liquified again and given to *anybody* whose life was dependent on a new blood supply. Blood from poor donors in dingy ghettos could save lives just as well as blood from Buckingham Palace could. "God has made of *one* blood all nations. . . ." In Christ, everybody is God's somebody.

In an economic sense, we are also bound together by our necessities and by our dependence on nature for all of our needs. The Chinese and the Russians have to get wheat from the United States. Our dry docks are building ships for the Arabs while they sell oil to us.

When my brother was staying in the heart pavilion of a downtown New York hospital to recover from his myocardial infarction, an Arab sheik from a nation that meets our need for oil was in the next room, flown over here to recover from his heart ailment and to use our top flight surgery. We need each other.

We are all children of one Father. We have the same needs and drives and urges, the same hungers and the same cravings. All people want *security*; all people want to feel *appreciated*; nobody wants to see his or her child go to bed *hungry* or his or her parents brought to *humiliation* in old age. This is *universal*. Everybody feels a little rhythm in the soul when happy children are at play, and everyone feels sorrow when dark, grey clouds hide the light of life in death.

One reason why black people have clung so tenaciously to Jesus, despite the apostasy and failure of Christians in acknowledging our human kinship and despite Christians' exploitation of one another through slavery, colonialism, and rank racism, is that blacks have found in Jesus the authentic, transcendent God incarnate, above and beyond race and clan and class. In truth we are one human family. Everybody is God's somebody.

And black people have the same needs that all people have, even though, as Paul Laurence Dunbar said, we wear a mask.

> We wear the mask that grins and lies.
> It hides our cheeks and shades our eyes.
> This debt we pay to human guile; with
> torn and bleeding hearts we smile. . . .[1]

[1] Paul Laurence Dunbar, "We Wear the Mask," in *The Complete Poems of Paul Laurence Dunbar* (New York: Dodd, Mead & Company, Inc., 1980).

Behind that mask we have the deep awareness of our full humanity. We are all basically alike even though some of us hide our real selves. Moreover, deep down inside the breast of every person there is a God-hunger, a need to know the Creator, the Father of all humankind, the Grand Architect of the universe, the Spirit of the living God. Of all the ways in which our common humanity is manifest, our common need to know God is the strongest evidence of our kinship. And black people have the same hunger to know God despite the awful way in which God has been represented in racist churches.

Come closer now and see that if God has indeed made of one blood all nations, then all of us are of *equal worth* in the sight of God. We may try to classify and stratify people on the basis of color, family name, hair texture, education, and money, but in God's sight the wealthiest aristocrat is no better than a poor little girl in the hollows of the Ozarks, with her nose running and her hair disheveled. The Bible says, "man looks on the outward appearance but the Lord looks at the heart."

Church people for far too long committed the grievous sin of being comfortable while dignity was being stripped from God's children. You see, it takes God, with an all-seeing eye, who never slumbers or sleeps to know why the Queen of England got to be queen and why the little girl from the Ozarks is there with the dirty nose. In God's sight we are equal.

Some of us have been party to a grand deception. Some persons have pretended to be inferior. In order to survive, some folk have had to *act* like they were less than others; some have had to *assume* a role of inferiority. And some have indeed been convinced of their inferior status! I remember being in the airport in Calcutta sometime ago. I saw a sweeper, an "outcast," as he crawled around the floor with a few straws held together, sweeping. I observed him, but I kept moving about freely. Suddenly I saw him leap. His shadow had crossed my shadow, and he had been taught that his shadow wasn't good enough to cross anybody's shadow.

The social costs of human degradation have been astronomical. It has not been easy or inexpensive to do this to people. *Black folk* have had to shuffle, scratch, and deceive to make it. We have all seen our parents say and do things they would never do or say except to keep food in the refrigerator, some soup on the stove, a roof over our heads, and something put aside for a rainy day. Have mercy! They suffered more than we ever knew.

This is the main lesson that we must get across to many black youth today. Before we do anything else, we must convince them that no matter how the society perceives them or treats them, they are God's precious children. We must convince them that they are loved with an infinite love and that when Jesus went to his cross, it was for the oppressed and forgotten people of the *whole* world. Thank God some do know that. Everybody is God's somebody. "God has made of one blood all nations. . . ."

You see, if you believe in that all-encompassing love, you won't let anybody shoot heroin in your arm; you won't let your mind be taken from you; you won't destroy your life; you won't drive a knife in another person's body; you won't be content in poor housing; you won't be satisfied with low skills, with a bad education, with garbage in your streets, or with politicians that are cold and indifferent. But, first, you've got to know deep down inside that you are a child of the King, that God is your Father, and that Jesus is your elder brother. And Paul recognized this as the best text he could find for his inaugural address, planting the gospel amid the philosophers of Athens, "God has made of one blood all nations. . . ."

The mute, persistent condition that underlies high crime statistics and the drug culture is self-rejection. Before persons can allow themselves to be subject to repeated arrests and intermittent jail terms, enslaved by drugs and its accompaniments, they must first give themselves a low self-estimate. The pride and self-respect that normally make us immune to these horrors must first be destroyed and laid aside.

Several generations of blacks suffered constant insults and abuses that were *intended* to destroy pride and self-respect, but they prayed their way through it all. God shielded them with a "wall of fire." We cannot accept injustices inflicted on others, and we will not participate in the infliction of such injustices ourselves. We become sensitive to our own involvement in injustice, whether direct and overt or subtle, indirect, or covert. We cultivate a righteous indignation at the sight of any action that denies persons their God-given dignity and worth.

In the 1950s and 1960s the nation developed a raised consciousness on the subject of injustice. The Supreme Court led the way with the 1954 school-desegregation decision; Martin Luther King, Jr., stirred up further concern with his crusades; the students added more impetus with their sit-in movement, and university students revolted against the Vietnam involvement of our country. In the wake of these movements a twentieth-century reconstruction occurred, and laws were passed in rapid succession, with the dynamic leadership of Congressman Adam Clayton Powell and many others, to refine the intention of the Constitution and to reaffirm the sublime promises of the Declaration of Independence.

But in the 1980s, twenty years later, a new consensus has emerged, supported by a strange view of Christianity that ignores the equality of persons before God and that treats with contempt all notions of fairness and equality of opportunity. A coalition of super-rich reactionaries, "convenient" evangelists, segregationists, anti-Semitists, anti-blacks, anti-poor, anti-women and anti-weak and anti-powerless, and old-fashioned bigots have conspired to undo all of the gains of the sixties.

But it will not be easy. Too many people have found out that everybody is God's somebody!

Victor Hugo said, "Greater than all the armies of the world is the power of an idea whose time has come." It is obvious to everyone that these are not the best days for the cause of justice in America, but the idea of justice is here and it is more powerful than marching armies. People can destroy affirmative action, but they cannot stifle that sense of worth that has been discovered and let loose among oppressed people. It is an idea whose time is here, now.

Finally, in a positive sense, when we believe that God has made us all of one blood, that belief becomes the foundation for the building of a true, genuine, and lasting community among all people, one that rises above race and clan, one that extends beyond tongue and nation, one that embraces the whole human family. Such a community comes about in the hearts and minds of persons and cannot be created by government or established by decree. It cannot be established by the state or denied by the state. Its charter is what Paul proclaimed in Athens, "*God* has made of one blood all nations. . . ."

One day during my tour as director of the Peace Corps in Nigeria, a young volunteer whose background was upper-middle class, came to Lagos to invite me to her site in Ogbomosho to see a library she had built and had stocked with book donations from Cleveland. So one day my assistant and I took off to see her project. What she had not told us was that in that city was a Yoruba chief who had graduated from my alma mater fifty years prior and who had been a schoolmate of an uncle of mine.

When we arrived, my assistant and I stood there on the one side—a young Jewish social worker from New York City and a black Baptist from Virginia; on the other side to welcome us stood a young white Oberlin graduate from Shaker Heights, Ohio, and an old Yoruba chief with deep tribal marks carved in his cheeks, who had been sent to a black college in Virginia by white Southern Baptists before World War I. And the center of our fellowship was our concern for the young Nigerians of Ogbomosho, not our color, our age, our education, our race, or our social status. We were as diverse as four persons could be, but we were locked together by our conviction that "God has made of one blood all nations. . . ."

Thank God, Christians have this test of their religion, namely, the convictions that we have a common Father and that our fellowship is the outgrowth of our faith. Thank God also that our fellowship, therefore, can become the nucleus of a wider, richer, deeper community among all peoples. This is not something to be grasped or sought after. As we live out our faith, it is as sure to follow as the seasons.

We the Christian community should have held our heads in shame when we found a so-called "Christian" university pleading to hold onto a federal tax exemption while it violated the Constitution, the Bill of Rights, the Declaration of Independence, the teachings of Christ, the strong message of the prophets, the Supreme Court decisions, and the witness of nature, history, and the highest scholarship for the past one hundred years, by practicing racial separation in the name of Jesus. What a denial of Christ while clinging to the outmoded mores of the past! How can a preacher proclaim in the name of the Lord of love and spew such hatred? When we see this kind of behavior, it becomes more urgent than ever to echo the theme of Paul in Athens, "God has made of one blood all nations. . . ."

A new world is waiting out there to be ushered in, a new condition among men and women waiting to pierce the gray clouds of our hate, our greed, our narrow nationalism, and our childish preoccupation with our own importance. What a privilege for preachers to echo the refrain with power and deep conviction: "Everybody is God's somebody!"

God has something better for us that will make slavery, racism, war, and nuclear stockpiling look like a nightmare, but we must begin where Paul began in Athens, "God has made of one blood all nations. . . ." And from this grand premise we then rebuild our attitudes, redesign our strategies, redefine our goals, and reorder our priorities to conform to the will of God. Then it will start making sense to us to beat our swords into plowshares and our spears into pruning hooks; then we will understand why starving children everywhere should be fed; then it will become a pure delight to see the walls of racism come tumbling down and a kingdom of love and righteousness rise among us.

Finding Our Margin of Freedom

Samuel D. Proctor

Galatians 3:1-29

The epistle to the Galatians has been called the Magna Carta of the Christian faith. It has been looked upon as the document that spells out the final break that Paul the Apostle made with the religion of his people, Judaism, and the clear origin of Christianity as a separate movement. Throughout Paul's first and second preaching tours he had preached in synagogues, talking with Jews about their Messiah, Jesus. But in the Galatian epistle he is making the case that anybody, not just the Jews, can be a Christian. "In Jesus Christ," Paul says, "neither circumcision availeth any thing, nor uncircumcision; but faith which worketh by love." A person does not have to be circumcised into Judaism first in order to be a Christian.

Paul had found out that some of the converts were not willing to trust Christ to be their full salvation, to cover their sin entirely, or to be adequate to empower them to all righteousness. They had accepted Christ, but they had held onto their loyalty to the Torah, the Jewish law, also. They took no chances. Paul, they thought, might have promised them too much, and they wanted to be sure! They accepted Christ, but they brought their synagogue membership along with them, just in case.

I recall that once I was interviewing a young minister to be our assistant pastor. As a part of the interview I asked him, "What do you think of Paul's Letter to the Galatians?" He frowned and said, "I didn't know that this was going to be a Bible quiz!" I moved on to other matters, but the interview was finished. If he did not understand Galatians, in my view, his training was far too shallow, for Galatians is central to our faith.

It is in Galatians that Paul says, ". . . I live; yet not I, but Christ liveth in me. . . ." It is in Galatians that he says, ". . . let us not be weary in well doing: for in due season we shall reap, if we faint not." In Galatians he says, "Be not deceived; God is not mocked: for whatsoever a man soweth, that shall he also reap." In Galatians he declares, "There is neither Jew nor Greek, there is neither bond nor free, there is neither male nor female; for ye are all one in Christ Jesus."

Galatians is the liberating epistle, setting believers free from the demands; the requirements; the proscriptions; the long list of rules about dress, food, travel, cooking, making sacrifices, and dealing with strangers. And in their place, it presents Christ as the all-sufficient Savior and the Holy Spirit as our divine energy and power. ". . . The fruit of the Spirit is love, joy, peace, longsuffering, gentleness, goodness, faith, meekness, temperance: against such, there is no law." So Christ is all you need. You don't need to hang on to anything else.

He wrote this to them because they had their doubts; and he dealt with their doubts straightforwardly: "Stand fast therefore in the liberty wherewith Christ hath made us free, and be not entangled again with the yoke of bondage." Now, he did not mean for them to go wild with their new freedom. They were free from the old rules, but they were captive to Christ and his Spirit. And he warned them: ". . . Ye have been called unto liberty; only use not liberty for . . . the flesh, but by love, serve one another. For all the law is fulfilled in one word, even in this; Thou shalt love thy neighbour as thyself."

Well, freedom is a frightening thing. We all want it, but it has its obligations and responsibilities. When a child is finally set free at eighteen or twenty-two, she or he finds out that it is different being on one's own. And many of them end up back in the nest. Freedom overwhelmed them. If you ask some of the leaders of the young nations like Trinidad, Jamaica, Sri Lanka, Zimbabwe, Nigeria, or Kenya, they will tell you that they are happy to have their independence, their freedom, but this freedom and this independence do not automatically create a strong country. Freedom is only the beginning. Then come the obligations and the responsibilities, the discipline and sacrifice. I have had friends who wanted to go into business on their own and be "free," but with that freedom came problems of maintaining cash flow, keeping goods well stocked, supervising the help, doing the paper work, paying the taxes, meeting the payroll, recovering from robbers, and giving credit to friends and kinfolk. It was freedom, but, oh, brother!!

Everyone has something from which he or she would like to be free. Most often it is freedom from some control exerted over one's life. America fought for freedom from England; blacks have fought for freedom from slavery and white supremacy; women have fought for freedom from male chauvinism; and we all want to be free from rising taxes.

Paul's problem was trying to get the young church members, the new Christians, to trust Christ to guide and sustain them as they assumed their freedom from the requirements of Judaism. And they were having a rough time.

Let us hasten to acknowledge that no one is ever entirely free. As long as we live in this world, we will be obligated in some sort of way; we can never be absolutely free. Just being alive obligates us to care for our physical and health needs. If we belong to a family unit, there are obligations to be carried constantly; if we have a job of any kind, we are limited and not entirely free.

Moreover, simply because we are human, we are bound also by our inheritance: the kind of home training we had; the kind of education that was afforded us; the amount of security, of warmth, and of feeling wanted that we were given as children; the talents we possess that we were encouraged to develop. Many of us are still enslaved by a wasted youth, and we spend hours wondering what life would have been like had we been given a better start. We are all bound in some way or another.

Paul is assuring us that Christ can show us how to find the freedom that we have available after everything else has been added up. A margin of freedom is always left. The people he preached to had been reared in synagogues, brought up under the law, raised in homes with long traditions; but he showed them the freedom available to them to outlive this background, to rise above their past, to unhinge their lives from their traditions, and to take on Christ and newness of life. And no matter what it is that binds you or me, Christ can show us the margin of freedom we have left, that inner sanctuary of the soul that God holds inviolate, where we have some power to choose, and we can turn that over to Christ and find the freedom we never thought we had.

Paul spoke from experience. He, too, had been bound and enslaved by his past. He was a young rabbi so violently against Christ that he set out to murder Christians. When writing to the Philippians, a church very close to his heart, he said that he had been, "Circumcised the eighth day, of the stock of Israel, of the tribe of Benjamin, an Hebrew of the Hebrews; ... a Pharisee, ... persecuting the church, ... blameless. But what things were gain to me I count loss for Christ." He changed. In Christ he found the power to use his freedom, and he changed. He said, "I can do all things—all things, through Christ who strengtheneth me."

And we can, too. It does not matter where we were born, what kind of rearing we had, who our friends were, what people did to us, what kinds of names we were called, what kind of trouble we once got into, how low we sank, or how far behind we fell. When we add it all up, we still have some options left, we still have some choices that we can make. There is a margin of freedom that God guarantees to all of us, and with Christ we can find it and use it.

Come now and see that when we find our margin of freedom, we can use it to outlive our past. Christ will give us the power. I recall being in Florida not long ago, visiting one of its fine universities, and after I had talked with students, there was a reception.

As I stood around talking, I noticed a young lady who was closer to me every time I looked up. Within minutes she was exactly in front of me, with her fingers locked together, whirling her thumbs, and innocently standing on the edge of her shoe soles, relaxed. "Where are you from?" I asked.

She said, "You mean where was I born? Exmore, Virginia."

"Well, that's a long way from here. What are you doing here?"

She explained that she was born in a migrant labor camp.

Her family traveled for most of the year, harvesting whatever was in season: beans and tomatoes in New Jersey, corn in Virginia, apples in upstate New York, potatoes on Long Island, tobacco in Connecticut, cotton in South Carolina, and oranges in Florida. They made their home on buses and trucks, staying on the roads between harvest seasons.

Among migrant laborers the children get very little schooling. The children are always rejected and isolated by the communities they happen to be near. But here she was, a graduate student, from that background. She said it was worse than that; when she was a teenager, unmarried, she bore a child. Her grandmother left the migrant group and settled in a small New Jersey town to rear the child until she could take over.

She was majoring in speech pathology and nearing the completion of her master's degree. She asked if my school had a doctoral program in speech pathology. I promised to look into it and send her the materials.

How had she gotten this far from a pregnant teenager on a migrant labor bus? Well, while working in the groves in Florida, she was spotted by a visiting teacher-counselor as a person of potential. This counselor helped her to find her margin of freedom. After all the elements of her awful background had been added up, the margin was there. She took a test, acquired her high school diploma, entered college on loans and grants, finished with a good record, was given more help to do her master's, and is now in a major university in the South pursuing her doctor's degree in speech pathology. She had found her margin of freedom. Paul said, "Stand fast therefore in the liberty wherewith Christ hath made us free."

What is binding you? What is holding you hostage? Have you found your margin of freedom? Are you a slave to your past? Are you a slave to alcohol? to drugs? to a bad temper? to an inferiority feeling about yourself? to your guilt and unforgiven sin that you will not confess to God? What is binding you?

We have the capacity to break the fetters that bind us. It is that bundle of human attributes that all of us have: our extraordinary power to think, to reason, to remember; our miraculous nervous system and the "big" brain that elevates us above behavior by instinct to behavior that we select from a range of choices; our creative powers of imagination that enable us to know persons through literature and to enjoy places and events that lie beyond our own experience. We are wondrously and marvelously made. We have the capacity to make tools, to invent ways of reaching the planet Venus, to write poems, to compose symphonies, to conquer diseases, to create community, to rid the world of war, hunger, and ignorance. And when we add it all together, it amounts to a veto power over the conditioners, the accumulated restraints that prevent us from reaching toward higher standards, from revising our values, from examining new career opportunitites, from throwing off a destructive relationship, from quitting a suicidal habit, from making a new beginning toward a strong and vital faith. We are equipped adequately enough, but we need the spiritual energy, the power, the release, the motivation, the spiritual rebirth that Christ provides. His leadership in our lives, when it is acknowledged, accepted, and gladly received, draws us into the orbit of God's inexhaustible power. Indeed, we can do all things through Christ who strengthens us.

Often we sit back and call other people lucky and ascribe their success to "contacts" and "influence." But in Christ we have the best contact there is: access to the power and love of God. "Stand fast therefore in the liberty wherewith Christ hath set us free."

Come and see that there is another secret to this. Once you have found your margin of freedom and have begun to explore it, you will find that it grows. It expands. The more you learn to exercise your freedom to make new choices for your life and engage the power of Christ, the larger the freedom gets. You forget where the boundaries were.

Working with young people for over thirty-five years as pastor and college teacher and administrator has rewarded me with some truly prize experiences. One day a handsome young man came to see me to sell me some books. I picked up somehow that he was not a "real" book salesman, that his heart was not in it. As he was about to leave, I asked him to sit back down. I told him of my suspicion and he confessed that he was only selling books to find himself and to make some money in the meantime. So I pressed on, "What would you do if you had your 'druthers'?" He said, "I would be an orthopedic surgeon. Why? What are you going to do about that?" He sounded annoyed.

I inquired about his background, the courses he had taken,

the grades earned, and how much he was willing to suffer and to endure in order to become an orthopedic surgeon. Everything he told me was promising. So I called the medical school people and laid the case before them. They advised some summer courses, a review of his grades, the medical school admission's test, and a few other requirements. He met them all. Within four years the young book salesman was an M.D., and he still had some freedom left. He went to Los Angeles, did a residency, won some prizes and certificates of recognition, and finished his speciality in orthopedic surgery. What else? He is now set up in the San Francisco Bay area of California. It is there, a margin of freedom, waiting for us to find it and use it.

This is not easy to do if we try it alone. Those old conditioners, those old habits, that old reputation, that old self-image are always around to tie us down and hold us back. But Paul said that if "any man be in Christ Jesus, he is a new creature. The old things are passed away, and all things are new." What a promise! This newness awaits us. We don't have to drag old habits, a bad disposition, a feeling of defeat, or a destructive animosity all through life. Christ gives us the freedom to overcome all of that. Thanks be to God.

Unfortunately, some of us who talk about Christ's freedom professionally have not found it ourselves, really. Recently I was in a conference with church leaders where the issues at hand and the demands laid upon us required our very best efforts. Everywhere I turned I discovered that I was involved in very heavy discussions. One day while at lunch, between sessions, I found myself deep in a debate with a bright young theologian teaching in one of our fine seminaries. He is a Christian, a faithful disciple, and a well-trained theologian, but he had not found the freedom to outgrow his boyhood racial stereotypes. He said to me, in making a point, "Oh, come on, Sam; you know that black preachers have a peculiar way of interpreting the Bible." Black preachers? What a category! All the way from Howard Thurman, Gardner Taylor, and Benjamin Mays to some who just started preaching with no preparation morally, intellectually, or spiritually—like some white preachers.

I asked, "How can you lump us all together on the basis of color? You must have some black preacher stereotype in mind." He apologized, and I kept him right there to help him look for other vestiges of racist thought that had clung to him and limited his usefulness as an interpreter of God's word.

The things that enslave us can be quite subtle, but Christ helps us. His love, his character, his compassion, his guidance, his truth will save us from the deceit, the confusion, and the conflict that hinder us. It is *his* freedom not just license, *his* freedom not mere promiscuity, *his* freedom not some sly rationalizations. And it is the finest discovery that one can make: finding one's margin of freedom.

Finally not only do we discover that we have this freedom and that it grows and expands as we use it, but we find out further that it is not just freedom *from* something but also freedom *for* something. It is not just an unshackling but an elevation. We are not just loose; we soar.

After slaves fought for their freedom and the abolition of slavery was accomplished in 1865, some of them walked right back into slavery. It was not *called* slavery, but it was the same existence. They were free on the books but not free in their minds and hearts. Some others were free in mind, free in spirit, and free in heart long before they were free on the books. And when the freedom bells rang and the whistles blew and jubilee songs filled the air, they took flight and left their old identities behind.

The freedom that Christ gives us is impelled by his Spirit, and this means freedom for a richer, fuller life; freedom for high spiritual adventure; freedom for participation in a new community of other souls who have found their freedom, too.

I have a friend, Martin England, a retired white South Carolinian who grew up in the thickness of unrelenting racist thought and behavior. Things are very different now; because of his age, one need not guess what the atmosphere was like in his formative years. He told me of an experience that he had that reveals the margin of freedom that he has found.

After retiring as a missionary in Asia, he had become an agent for a Baptist minister's pension and insurance plan. And it struck him one day to inquire if Martin Luther King, Jr., was covered by such a plan. He found that King had been too engrossed in his cause to give much thought to such a matter, so my friend took off to find him and to get him enrolled. He had a feeling that King was exposed to some unusual risks and that such a plan was urgent for him and his young family.

Well, this tall, thin, gray-haired, white South Carolinian began tracking King from place to place, but King's aides protected him from all such persons who looked like salesmen, unsolicited advisors, and unidentified white "friends" who wanted to see him. No one knows what this soft-spoken, modest man endured trying to elbow his way through those 200-pound, heavy-voiced protectors that surrounded King at the height of his popularity. But Martin England pursued his task like a man possessed; and after months of travel, rejection, embarrassments and put offs, he finally got to King. King signed. And shortly thereafter his young life was ended while he was with the garbage men in Memphis.

What kept this white, South Carolina–born Christian, Martin England, following King to get him enrolled? What enabled him to defy the prevailing mores and attitudes? What gave him this transcendence over the social structures and the constraints in the culture? What kept him taking his case from town to town to help Martin Luther King, contrary to the expected patterns of behavior for one in his place? The answer is that some indeed have found their margin of freedom. And it is a freedom that Christ controls. It lifts us to higher and higher heights while on this pilgrim journey, and in the end, when this life is over, because we are free in him, it will be like the old folks used to sing:

> One bright morning when this life
> is o'er, I'll fly away,
> I'll fly away, Oh Glory, I'll fly away.[1]

---

[1] From "I'll Fly Away."

Go On

William D. Watley

Joshua 1:1-5

One of those matchless points of genius and beauty of the Bible is found in its capacity to be profoundly simple. This is to say, often the Bible speaks in simple language and in a simple way of complex and multifaceted issues, deep and profound mysteries, and great challenging questions, which leave man's intellect searching and groping. The Bible has a misguiding simplicity. It often says what it wants to say in such a clear and easy way that if you are not careful, you will be so unmoved and unimpressed that you will fail to see the deeper meaning which often lies within those words.

When Elijah fled from Jezebel in fear to Mount Horeb, he expected God to come as some great cataclysmic and catastrophic force in wind, earthquake, and fire. But God came to him simply—as a still, small voice that asked a simple but searching question, "What doest thou here, Elijah?"

After David had caused the death of Uriah, the husband of his lover Bathsheba, the prophet Nathan trapped him, not with any fine point of legal jurisprudence but with a simple parable. Nathan simply said, "There were two men in a certain city, one was rich and the other poor. As would be expected, the rich man had many flocks and herds. The poor man, however, had only one ewe lamb that he had bought. The poor man's lamb was like a member of the household. It ate of his morsels, drank from his cup and lay in his bosom as if it were his daughter. One day an out-of-town guest came to lodge in the rich man's house. The rich man, however, was unwilling to take one of his many flock to serve to his guest, and so he took the poor man's lamb and killed it. Tell me, king, what do you think of such a person?" David replied, "As the Lord lives, such a man who has been so cruel, so selfish, and so callous deserves to die." Then Nathan told David, "I have news for you—you are the man."

When Nicodemus came to the Master with the problem of unfulfilled religion, the Master did not search the Mishnah or any of the rabbinical writings; rather, he spoke to Nicodemus in very simple language. He simply said, "Your problem, Nicodemus, is that you need to be born again." The Master's language was so simple that Nicodemus almost missed the point, for he replied, "How can a man be born when he is old? Can he enter a second time into his mother's womb and be born?" Jesus said, "Nicodemus, you don't understand. Unless an individual is born of water and the Spirit, then that person cannot enter the kingdom of God. That which is born of the flesh is flesh, and that which is born of the Spirit is spirit."

When Jesus spoke about the suprarational inexplainable nature and mystery of God's grace and the love that is shown toward all of God's children, our Lord spoke simply. He told of a prodigal son who, after leaving home, came to himself in a hog pen one day and returned to a father's forgiving love. When Jesus explained the meaning of the incarnation, the compassion behind it, and the purpose of his mission, he said, "I'm like a good shepherd. I know my own, and my own know me. The good Shepherd lays down his life for his sheep."

And so God is with us. When we reach those points of crisis in our lives when we don't know what to do, where to go, or where to turn; when all around us are questions but no answers; when it seems as if our backs are up against the wall or as if we are standing at the edge of a cliff, God often comes to us not in the profundity of lightning but in the simplicity of a still, small voice. And even though God remains an enigma and somewhat of a mystery, he often speaks simply, in language that we can understand. When our spirits are low, our minds confused, our hearts burdened, our souls weary, God often speaks a word of persistence. And when we wonder how we shall persist, God speaks a word of assistance. The message from our text is a case in point.

When God spoke the words of the text to Joshua, the children of Israel, the children of the promise, were probably experiencing an inner crisis. For you see, Moses was dead. Moses—who had been the one man courageous enough to confront Egypt's power structure, armed with nothing but his staff and an edict from God and a directive to Pharaoh (who thought himself to be somewhat divine): "Let my people go"—that Moses was dead. Moses—who had secured Israel's emancipation from Egypt and had guided the people for forty years in the wilderness; whose prayers had brought them manna from heaven when they were hungry and water from a rock when they were thirsty—that Moses was dead. Moses—who, when all seemed lost and everything seemed hopeless as Pharaoh's army charged from behind and the Red Sea appeared as a watery grave in front, had stretched forth his staff and the waters rolled back and dry land appeared as a path through the troubled deep—that Moses was dead. Moses—who could go alone upon a mountain and talk with God while the rest of the Israelites stood back, fearing that if they even touched the mountain where Moses stood and talked, they would die; whom the Israelites had learned to look to and lean upon in periods of crisis; who towered before them as a pillar of strength—that Moses was now dead.

The loss of a leader of Moses' stature is bad enough, but when the loss occurs at a critical stage in a people's history, when it occurs at the turning point of a people's life, that loss is magnified. You see, the children of Israel were about to embark on the second phase of their journey toward freedom; that phase was the capturing of the land of Canaan. They now stood looking over the Jordan River, standing between the slavery of Egypt and the freedom of Canaan, thinking about the challenges, the battles, the struggles that were before them, and knowing that whatever they faced this time, they would have to face without the seasoned and fatherly leadership of Moses.

The God who first spoke to Moses through a burning bush

in the desert on the backside of a mountain and bid him to go to Egypt; the God who had guided him, directed him, and upheld him during all those moments of crisis in the wilderness; the God about whom David said, "shall neither slumber nor sleep," was far from being dead. This same God spoke to Joshua, the second in command who would now become the first in command, to Joshua, Moses' lieutenant, and said: "Now look, son. I know that your heart is heavy. I know that you will feel keenly the loss of Moses, especially since the mantle of leadership has been placed upon your shoulders. But no matter how much you grieve, Moses is dead. And when you finish crying and throwing accolades upon him, he'll still be dead. Nothing is going to change that. So lift up your head and look around you. There's still a job to be done; there's still a charge to be kept; there's still a responsibility to be discharged. So get up from where you are and go on. The land that I promised your ancestors remains to be conquered; the wilderness has yet to be cleared; the cities still must be built. So arise, you and all your people, and go over the Jordan into the land of promise. Every place that the soles of your feet shall tread upon will be yours. Every piece of land that your eyes shall rest upon from the rising of the sun to the going down of the same will be yours. No man shall be able to stand against you all the days of your life. So arise and go on.

"Now don't think it's going to be easy. Sometimes you'll give your best, and your best won't seem good enough, and you'll begin to wonder if you really are called to this work, but just go on. Sometimes you'll go out of your way to help folk, and the very ones you've tried to help the most will be the first to talk about you when your back is turned, but just go on. Sometimes when you try to stand for the right, it will seem as if you are standing by yourself, but don't worry about it; just go on. Sometimes the opposition will seem too great; sometimes it will seem as if the system will destroy you, but just go on. In spite of high mountains, go on; in spite of deep valleys, go on; in spite of wide rivers, go on. In spite of the betrayal of friends, the rejection of relatives, the railings of the enemy, just go on. Sometimes folk will get mad at you and fight what you are trying to do for them; sometimes your staunch supporters will become discouraged and fall by the wayside; sometimes folk will get mad and quit, but you just go on."

As God spoke to Joshua, so God speaks to us. When we are overwhelmed by life's problems and life's setbacks; when we have tried to be good pastors, good Christian men or women, good husbands or wives, devoted sons or daughters, responsible young persons and it seems as if the devil has made a shambles of our work, our lives, our homes, or our marriages; when the responsibilities are great, odds against us overwhelming, and we are most aware of our own weaknesses and shortcomings, God speaks to us simply, with a word of persistence; "Don't give up. Keep on fighting. Keep on trying. Just go on." In spite of the stumbling blocks thrown in our way, and the ditches that have been dug, and the snares that have been set, just go on anyhow. Go on, even though many false prophets shall arise and deceive many and lead many astray, even though iniquity shall abound and the love of many shall wax cold, you just go on anyhow because the person who endures to the end shall be saved.

I know sometimes we feel like saying, "How can I go on, Lord? I'm all alone; it's just me alone. The challenge is too great, the opposition is too powerful, and I'm too weak and powerless." It is at this moment that God speaks to us the word of assistance. God says to us what was said to Joshua, ". . . as I was with Moses, so I will be with thee: I will not fail thee nor forsake thee." What God was saying to Joshua is, "You don't understand who it is that's talking to you. I am the one who causes to be what is. Before there was a 'when' or a 'where' or a 'then' or a 'there,' I was. It was I who stepped out into the darkness into the blackness and bleakness of chaos and said, 'Let there be light.' It was I who spat out the seven seas, carpeted the earth with grass, dotted the hills with trees, and flung the stars throughout the Milky Way. I'm the one who told Abraham to go; I'm the one who stopped him from sacrificing Isaac; it was my angel that wrestled with Jacob all night long; you don't have to tell me what happened to Joseph in Egypt, for I was there! Whatever Moses did, he did not through his own cunning but through my wisdom, not by his own strength but by my power. And as I've been with others, as I've upheld others, as I've fed others, as I've led others, so I'll be with you. I will neither fail nor forsake you."

We can go on because God is our protector, because Christ is our traveling companion, because the Holy Ghost is our comforter and our guide. When our paths get blocked, our God will be a fence all around us, and when hellhounds are on our trail, he'll stand between them and us as a pillar of fire. I'm a witness that if you just stretch out on God's word and stand upon the promises of the Lord, he'll fight your battles, if you just keep still.

Therefore, no matter what happens from day to day, go on. No matter what foes appear in battle array, go on. No matter who tells you that you can't make it, you know in whom you have believed; so go on. When you have been falsely accused and are being persecuted for righteousness' sake; when jealous minds, vindictive spirits, petty souls, and unconverted hearts cast your name out as evil, trust God and go on. Go on because David has said, "'The steps of a good man are ordered by the LORD; and he delighteth in his way. Though he fall, he shall not be utterly cast down: for the LORD upholdeth him with his hand.' I once was young but now I'm old and during my life I've seen a lot of things. I've seen men play their political games with the lives of other men and the well-being of their families as if they were little boys playing with toys. I've seen friends betray friends. And I've seen men use others to advance their own personal ends. I've seen just about all of the mean tricks that men and women perpetrate on their brothers and their sisters. I know about them because I've played some of them myself. But in all of my years one thing I have not seen—I've never seen the righteous forsaken or their children begging bread."

Sometimes, like Paul, we may ask, "Lord, how can I go on when I have this thorn in my flesh and in my soul that keeps me from doing what I want to do and being what I ought to be? Three times I have besought you in prayer and asked that this burden be removed from my life." We are then given the same message that was given to Paul, "Go on because my grace is sufficient for you and my strength is made perfect in your weakness."

If we go on depending upon sufficient grace, trusting in the promises of God, looking unto Jesus, the author and perfecter of our faith, and being kept by power divine, one of these old days we will reach the Promised Land. We will cross the Jordan River; Jericho's wall will fall down before us; and we will claim the prize of the high calling in Christ Jesus our Lord.

Believe

William D. Watley

Genesis 15:6; Genesis 22:1-15

It has been said that a man is what he eats. Someone else has said that a man is what he reads. Still another has said that a man is what he thinks. Proverbs says, "As a man thinketh in his heart, so is he." To these axiomatic statements that identify the essence of a person's being I would add another which says that a person is what he or she believes. You are not only what you consume physically or what you conceptualize or internalize mentally, but you are also what you believe in your heart.

If you believe you can, then you can; if you believe you cannot, then you won't be able. Everything we do, from the most simple acts to the most complex tasks, requires that we believe in ourselves and our abilities to perform. Before we can get out of bed or lift a fork or speak a word, before we can memorize a speech or learn a lesson or drive a car, before we can quit smoking or drinking or overeating or any other habit, we must first believe that we can. And if we don't have strength ourselves, then we must have enough faith to believe in God and in the power of Christ to help us do what we believe we cannot do for and by ourselves.

We are what we believe. If we believe that we are nobodies, then nobodies are all we will ever be.

Once when I was a very young preacher still in seminary and pastoring a church of about twenty members, an older minister asked me how I was doing. I told him that I was doing fine for a little preacher. The older minister looked at me and said, "Young man, if you consider yourself to be a little preacher, then a little preacher is all you will ever be." I had not lived long enough then to know that one's stature does not depend upon physical size or the size of one's office or church but upon what a person is on the inside. A big person in a little spot is still a much bigger person than a little person in a big spot.

No one can make you into a failure; you must do that yourself. No matter how many times you've tried and failed, you are never a failure until you begin to believe yourself to be and consider yourself to be a failure. As long as you don't give up, you can keep on trying. You'll hold your head up and bounce back no matter how many times you've been discouraged, frustrated, or disappointed. But once you give up on yourself, on God, on life, on other people, then failure is inevitable. For no person ever really starts failing until that person begins to fail from the inside out.

Malcolm X once said that this society's greatest crime against blacks was teaching us to hate ourselves. Self-hate, self-doubt, a lack of self-esteem and belief in self, a lack of self-respect and pride have been and continue to be some of our greatest obstacles to being a truly free and victorious people.

We've all heard the story of a white man who sold ice in the black community. A certain enterprising young black person observed what the man was doing and decided that he could go into business and do the same thing. He produced a quality product at a lower cost and even gave better service. Soon all of the black folk were buying their ice from this young man— all except one old lady. Try as he might, this young black man could not persuade the old lady to buy his ice. Finally, in exasperation, he asked her why she wouldn't give him her business. She replied, "Son, it has nothing to do with you personally, but I just believe that the white man's ice is just a little bit colder than yours."

As long as we believe that others' ice is colder; as long as we are on the treadmill of self-hate and self-doubt that causes us to disrespect, deprecate, and kill each other; as long as we mug, burglarize, terrorize, and "do in" each other; as long as we fail to believe in each other, then we will never be free. As long as we believe the lies about ourselves that a racist culture has told us and a racist educational system has perpetuated, then we will always be hewers of wood and drawers of water.

When we fail to believe in ourselves, we are an affront to the God who made us. You will remember that in the book of Numbers we read of a tragic incident that occurred while the Israelites were on their journey to the Promised Land. When they had reached Kadesh-barnea in the wilderness of Paran, Moses sent out twelve men to spy on and survey the Promised Land and bring back a report. Only Caleb and Joshua saw the land and encouraged the people to go forward. The other ten spies looked at the land of promise but paid more attention to their opposition. They said, "The land is good, and it flows with milk and honey just as we were told. But the cities are high and fenced in, and the people who inhabit them are giants. 'We were in our own sight as grasshoppers, and so we were in their sight.'" It was at this point that God told Moses to keep the children of Israel in the wilderness until that generation died out.

This was not the first time that the Israelites had complained and wanted to go back to Egypt. They had complained and wanted to return when their provisions had run short. They had complained at the banks of the Red Sea. This, God could abide. God could make a way through the Red Sea and God could give them manna to eat and provide water in a starving land. However, he could not make them believe in themselves— they had to do that of their own accord. And when those whom God had chosen refused to believe, then God raised up in the wilderness another generation.

When we stop believing, when we become cynical, we stymie and shackle the power of Christ in our own lives. When Jesus went home to Nazareth, he did not do any mighty works there— not because the power that had worked elsewhere would not work there, nor because he doubted his own abilities. The Scriptures tell us that Jesus did no mighty works in Nazareth because of the people's unbelief.

Abraham was a great man because he had a great faith. Our text tells us that Abraham "believed in the LORD; and he counted it to him for righteousness." Abraham believed God. He did not slay any giants as David did, or write any proverbs as did Solomon. Abraham believed God. He did not confront any pharaohs or dispense any laws as did Moses. Abraham simply believed God. He was not a learned scribe like Ezra or a great builder like Nehemiah. He did not have Samson's strength or Mordecai's political acumen. Abraham believed God. He did not command the sun to stand still as Joshua did or defeat any armies as Gideon did. He did not walk through any flames as did the three Hebrew boys Shadrach, Meshach, and Abednego, or spend any time in a lions' den as Daniel did. Abraham simply believed God. He did not dream any dreams as did Joseph or see any visions as did Ezekiel. Abraham believed God. He did not proclaim the Messiah's coming as did Isaiah or call forth fire from heaven as Elijah did. Abraham just believed God.

When God instructed him to pack up and journey to a land that he knew not but that would be given to his descendants, Abraham, a well-established and settled householder, believed God and went. When Abraham was told that he and his wife Sarah, a childless couple, would bear a child and that their descendants would be as numerous as the sands along the seashore and that through them all the nations of the earth would be blessed, Abraham believed God. Abraham saw himself and his wife Sarah grow far beyond childbearing years, but still he believed God. When Abraham was ninety-nine and Sarah was ninety, their son Isaac was born.

Let me just point out that miracles can still happen when you believe long enough and strong enough. The sick that folk have given up for dead, the sick that folk have pronounced as lifelong invalids can still be healed when we believe. Hezekiah lay upon his deathbed one day, body aching and racked with pain. Doctors and others had given up hope for him and had said it was just a matter of time before death came. But Hezekiah turned his face to the wall and cried out for mercy and healing, and God added fifteen years to his life.

Ways can still be made out of no ways when you believe. Those who seem lost forever can still be saved when you believe. Jesus does save to the uttermost. The prodigal son did come to himself in a pig pen one day and find his way back home. The adversary can still be conquered when you believe. All things are still possible if only we would believe.

One dreadful day when the Lord spoke to Abraham and told him to take Isaac—the son of his old age, his pride and joy and the crowning glory of his life, upon whom Abraham had placed his hopes for posterity, whose life Abraham cherished more than his own—when God told Abraham to take Isaac and sacrifice him, still Abraham believed. When Abraham left with Isaac and a few servants for Mount Moriah, nobody knew how heavy Abraham's heart was.

You need to understand that there's going to come a time in your life when your beliefs and everything you claim to stand for will be tested. There will come a time when your courage and faith will be strained to the breaking point, or so it will seem, and you will cry out, "Lord, how much more and how much longer?"

God had made such a request of Abraham, and Abraham felt that he could not share what he was about to do or what he was going through with anybody because he knew they wouldn't understand. Frankly, Abraham himself didn't understand, but still he believed God.

You need to understand that you're going to have to walk through some of life's valleys by yourself. Not even your closest companion or friend or loved one can do anything to help you. Sometimes, like the prophet of old, you must tread life's winepresses alone. When I was a boy, people used to sing:

> You've got to stand your test and judgment;
> You've got to stand it for yourself.
> Nobody else can stand it for you,
> You've got to stand it for yourself.[1]

It's terrible to feel alone, so alone that even the God whom you have been leaning upon seems like a distant stranger. For, there will be times when you pray that you won't get an answer that satisfies. And out of the depths of your distress you will cry out like Job, "Oh that I knew where I might find him! that I might come even to his seat!"

This was the heaviness that must have gripped Abraham's heart that day when God told him to sacrifice Isaac. Surely the Lord knew his heart. Everything that Abraham had been told to do he had done without murmur or complaint. The Lord had

---

[1] "Jesus Walked This Lonesome Valley."

to know how much he loved Isaac; so why would God not only take his son but also require Abraham to kill him with his very own hand? Abraham did not understand, but still he believed God.

Abraham believed God so much that when he began to build and prepare the altar and Isaac said, "Father, . . . behold the fire and the wood: but where is the lamb for a burnt offering?" Abraham believed God enough to reply, "God will provide a lamb for a burnt offering, my son."

Abraham bound his son, but at the moment Abraham raised his arm with knife in hand to slay Isaac, he felt a tug on his wrist and a voice called to him from heaven and told him, "Do your son no harm, for now I know that you fear God, seeing that you have not withheld your son, your only son from me." Abraham lifted up his eyes and, behold, he saw a ram behind him caught by its horns in the thicket. Abraham sacrificed the ram as a burnt offering instead of his son.

God always has a ram in the bush for those who are determined enough, who love him enough, to believe him in spite of everything and through it all. For God is still able to open doors that no one can shut and shut doors that no one can open. "He's the King of Kings and He's Lord of Lords; no man works like Him."

We all have heard the story of a ship that was caught in a storm so terrible that many of the passengers had put on life vests. It seemed as if at any moment the seaworthy vessel would capsize. As one of the passengers was scurrying around, he happened to see a little boy sitting in the middle of the dining room by himself, calmly and cheerfully playing with his toy truck, seemingly oblivious to the storm around him. The concerned passenger ran up to him and said, "Little fellow, you had better put on a life vest and find your parents. Don't you know how serious the storm is?" The little boy looked up at him and said, "Thank you, Mister, but I'm not worried because my daddy is the captain of the ship."

There may be some who wonder how you can keep on believing when everything is turning against you. There may be some who wonder how you can keep smiling when you're going through one of the worst storms in your life. There may be some who wonder how you can hold your head up and appear so strong when your whole world is crashing all around you and the very foundations of your life are being shaken. But if you know, in spite of what people say and do, that your heavenly Father is at the control panel of your life and that he has not lost either a passenger or a ship yet but has landed many a thousand, you can have a peace that passes understanding. You can say like Job, "Say what you will or may, but I'm going to keep on believing. I may not understand all that's happening, but I'm going to keep on believing. For 'though he slay me yet shall I trust in him!' For this I know: 'I know that my redeemer liveth and that He shall stand at the latter day upon the earth and though after my skin worms destroy this body, yet in my flesh shall I see God: whom . . . mine eyes shall behold and not another. . . .' "

Therefore, no matter what happens from day to day, keep on believing. Understand that for everything that happens, God has a reason. Somebody said:

> I trust in God wherever I may be,
> Upon the land or on the rolling sea,
> For, come what may, From day to day,
> My heav'nly Father watches over me.
>
> Chorus:
> I trust in God,—I know He cares for me
> On mountain bleak or on the stormy sea;
> Tho' billows roll, He keeps my soul,
> My heav'nly Father watches over me.[2]

[2]"My Heavenly Father Watches Over Me."

Standing for a Cause

William D. Watley

Daniel 3:16-18

Every person—whether male or female, old or young, black or white, rich or poor, educated or uneducated, professional or common laborer—ought to stand for something. Every person ought to live for something and possess some basic principles, beliefs, and convictions that he or she is willing to die for. At some point each person ought to be able to look in the face of personal aggrandisement or survival, political expediency, and that deceptive creature known as compromise and declare, "This far and no farther." If a number of us feel that our lives are empty of meaning and devoid of substance, the reason may very well be that we have no beliefs to guide us, no principles to which we have committed ourselves, and no convictions around which we have dared to shape our lives and upon which we have staked our future.

A poet once said:

> To every man there openeth
> A Way, and Ways, and a Way.
> And the High Soul climbs the High Way,
> And the Low Soul gropes the Low,
> And in between, on the misty flats,

The rest drift to and fro.
But to every man there openeth
A High Way, and a Low.
And every man decideth
The way his soul shall go.[1]

The trouble with most of us is that we are too fickle and we are afraid to commit ourselves too much to any one cause or course of action. Rather than commit ourselves to something that we are willing to back with our lives, our jobs, or other symbols of human security, we would rather drift along on the misty flats of indecision where we don't make any choices but allow others and circumstances to make decisions for us or on the misty flats of popularity where having people speak well of us means more than the integrity of our convictions or on the misty flats of convenience where we espouse a cause as long as our stand does not cost us anything or on the misty flats of "two-facedness" where we try to "run with the hares and holler with the hounds."

No one, however, appreciates a person who tries to stand on both sides of the fence or who talks out of both sides of the mouth. The biblical record is a continuing plea for the human spirit to be resolute and to stand for one thing or the other. Joshua told Israel: "Choose you this day whom you will serve, whether the gods your fathers served in the region beyond the River, or the gods of the Amorites in whose land you dwell; but as for me and my house, we will serve the Lord." On Mount Carmel Elijah asked the covenant people: "How long will you go limping with two different opinions? If the Lord is God, follow him; but if Baal, follow him." Our Lord and Savior Jesus Christ has said: "No man can serve two masters; for either he will hate the one and love the other, or he will be devoted to the one and despise the other." One of these days we are going to learn that, try as best and as much as we might, we cannot serve God and mammon.

Standing for a cause, however, can be risky business. The story of our text is the story of three young men who decided to stand for a cause and found themselves in a fiery furnace. One day Nebuchadnezzar, king of Babylon, who was caught up in an exaggerated sense of his own importance—which is

[1]John Oxenham, "The Ways," *Masterpieces of Religious Verse*, ed. James Dalton Morrison (New York: Harper & Row, Publishers, Inc., 1948), p.3.

always a dangerous attitude to have—decided that he would build a golden image of himself, which was ninety feet high and nine feet wide, and set it in the plain of Dura in the province of Babylon. Nebuchadnezzar directed that at the playing of the horn, pipe, bagpipe, lyre, harp and all kinds of music, every person was to bow down and worship the golden image; whoever refused to do so would be cast into a burning furnace. As could be expected, at the playing of the music everyone in the kingdom bowed to the image, with the exception of three young Jewish captives known as Shadrach, Meshach, and Abednego.

Some persons went to the king and said: "O King, you're a great king; you're the greatest king we have ever had. We haven't had an administration on this order before. You are kind to your subjects and your requests are not unreasonable or burdensome. You made a simple request that at the playing of the music every person bow down and worship the golden image, which is an appropriate tribute to your greatness. Well, those three youngsters that you have placed over the province of Babylon, those three Hebrew boys that you passed over some of us for, are refusing to obey your orders."

Let us never forget that there are always those who are ready to run to the king. On the job, in our communities, in our churches are always those who consider their personal mission to be that of reporting to the king on their brothers and sisters and colleagues in captivity. One of the greatest obstacles to the freedom of blacks has been those who "run to the king" in an effort to show loyalty when, in actuality, all they are showing is their cowardice and the fact that they cannot be trusted. For anyone who betrays his or her own will also betray others. Still, there are those who will do anything to curry favor and receive a few handouts.

During the period of antebellum slavery the blacks of Charleston, South Carolina, under the leadership of Denmark Vesey, had devised a brilliant plan to take over the town. However, that stratagem was never executed because at the last minute somebody "ran to the king" and told him about the plan.

Further, let us never forget that there are always those who envy where we are and what we have—no matter what it is or how little it is—and they don't mind going to the king, reporting everything we say or do so that they can get where we are or get what we have.

When Nebuchadnezzar heard of Shadrach, Meshach, and Abednego's refusal to bow, he flew into a rage and ordered them to appear before him. When we stand for a cause, we must be prepared to oppose those whom we consider to be important people—kings, queens, presidents, pastors, bishops, moderators, officers, so-called "church pillars," teachers, judges, and employers. Sometimes we must be prepared to lay our futures and our lives on the line for what we believe. That's why we need to be very sure that the cause that we're sacrificing all for is worth the risks we are taking and the price we are paying, for in this life there are all kinds of causes upon which to take a stand. We need to be very sure that the cause we are risking all for is not some passing fad but one which will stand the test of time.

If Calvary proved anything, it is that there are some things that still come out winners at the finishing line, no matter how aggressive evil may be. Goodness, justice, truth, righteousness, faith, and love will stand. Evil may crucify them on Friday, but God is able to raise them on Sunday. Black liberation, women's liberation, and the peace movement are just causes that deserve the support of thinking, socially conscious Christians. However, we must never forget that none of these movements can in and of themselves save our souls. That's why when I think of that which is basic, first, and ultimate to my life, I've decided to make Jesus my choice. It is only as one seeks first the kingdom of God and its righteousness that one is truly liberated to work in history and in one's existential situation for the justice that is intrinsic to Christ's vision of a fully consummated kingdom.

When the three Hebrews appeared before Nebuchadnezzar, he confronted them about their flagrant and willful violation of his orders. He said: "How could you embarrass me like this after all I've done for you? I placed you over one of my strongest provinces. I went against the advice of some of my most trusted counselors and appointed you over the province of Babylon, and what thanks do I get? All across this land at the sound of the music, people are bowing down—except you three in whose province the statue stands. Now let's just say that you didn't understand my orders. I'm going to give you one more chance.

If you agree to worship my image when you hear the sound of music, all is forgiven and forgotten. But if you still refuse to obey my order, then you will be cast into the fiery furnace, and who is the god that will deliver you out of my hands?"

Shadrach, Meshach, and Abednego said, "O Nebuchadnezzar, we have no need to answer you in this matter. The issue for us isn't even up for discussion or debate. If it be so, our God whom we serve—not just the God of our mothers and fathers and not simply the God of history but the God whom we serve— is able to deliver us out of your hand, O King." These three young men were able to take a stand, not just because their cause was right, noble, just, and worthy of risk but because they believed that God is able.

I'm convinced that most of us don't really believe that God is able. We would spend less time worrying if we really believed that God is able. We would spend less time setting people straight and telling folk off and trying to get even with those who have wronged us if we really believed that God is able to fight battles for those who trust. We wouldn't give up because of a doctor's diagnosis if we really believed that God is able to work miracles. We wouldn't give up on that wayward family member if we really believed that Jesus is able to save to the uttermost. We wouldn't give up on prayer so easily if we really believed that our God is "able to do exceeding abundantly above all that we ask or think, according to the power that worketh in us. . . ." This is the reason why we are afraid to take a stand for right—we really don't believe that God is able.

However, if we know God, we can take a few risks. We can say like Paul, "For the which cause I also suffer these things: nevertheless I am not ashamed: for I know whom I have believed, and am persuaded that he is able to keep that which I have committed unto him against that day." Our foreparents also believed that God is able, and that's why they could sing:

> I love the Lord: he heard my cries,
>   And pitied every groan:
> Long as I live, when troubles rise
> I'll hasten to his throne.[1]

We may not know how the king or queen will react or what they will say or do if we take our stand. We may not even know

[1] "I Love the Lord."

how our friends will treat us or relatives view us if we take a stand. But this one thing we know—God is able.

The three Hebrew boys proclaimed, "We know that our God is able to deliver us from the furnace. But if not, be it known unto you, O King, that we will not serve your gods or worship the golden image that you have set up." We must never forget that if one's cause is meaningful enough, then it is possible for death to lose its sting. It was because death had lost its sting that the Hebrew boys could face the fiery furnace, that Daniel could face the lions' den, that the early church could face hungry lions, that Paul could face Nero's chopping block. It was because death had lost its sting that Jesus could face Calvary. That's why he could pray in Gethsemane, ". . . Nevertheless not as I will, but as thou wilt."

There is something about a righteous cause that allows one to transcend the fear of death. A righteous cause is grounded in a God who is too wise to make a mistake and who works all things together for good for those who love the Lord and are called according to his purpose. Consequently, even if God doesn't answer prayers the way we might desire ("but if not"), we shall not bow down to the unrighteous edicts of a fallible king. Even if we are not delivered in this life, we will not forsake our faith; we will not worship at the altars of strange gods. Even in defeat we are going to love and trust the God we know.

When Nebuchadnezzar heard the witness of the Hebrew boys, he ordered that the furnace be heated seven times hotter than it normally was. Then he sent Shadrach, Meshach, and Abednego to what he believed was certain death. Because the furnace was so much hotter than usual, the flames slew those persons who carried the Hebrews to the door of the furnace.

You know, we must be careful about stoking the flames for somebody else because the flames can reach out and grab us. When I was a boy, I delighted in watching Frankenstein movies. However, I noticed that after the monster finished killing everybody else, he always turned on the person who created him and slew his creator. In the book of Esther we read that Haman had constructed a large gallows upon which he planned to hang Mordecai. However, Haman didn't know that God had placed Mordecai's niece Esther on the throne as queen for such a time as that. Consequently, Haman ended up hanging from the very gallows that he had constructed for Mordecai. The lies we tell on others, the gossip we spread on others, the dirt we do to others will come back to us.

Shadrach, Meshach, and Abednego fell, bound, into the flames of the furnace, but God took the heat out of the flames. Let us remember that we are not killed by the flames but by the heat in the flames. Sometimes God will allow us to be put in the fire, but he takes the heat out of the flames. He did it for the Hebrew boys, and he can do it for us. God took the heat out of the flame for Isaiah when God told him, ". . . Fear not, for I have redeemed you; I have called you by name; you are mine. When you pass through the waters I will be with you; and through the rivers, they shall not overwhelm you; when you walk through fire you shall not be burned, and the flame shall not consume you. For I am the Lord your God, the Holy One of Israel, your Savior."

One hymn writer said:

> When through fiery trials thy pathway shall lie,
> My grace, all sufficient, shall be thy supply:
> The flame shall not hurt thee: I only design
> Thy dross to consume, and thy gold to refine.[2]

God takes the heat out of the flames. What Nebuchadnezzar saw when he looked into the furnace was not three men bound but four persons walking around. The fourth had the appearance of the Son of God. Let us never forget that no furnace is so hot that it can keep God out. Let us never forget that we do not face the fiery furnaces of this life alone; the Lord is with us. He was the fourth person in the furnace with the Hebrew boys, the third person with Paul and Silas in prison, the second person with John on Patmos, and the first to conquer death. He reigns forevermore as king over all of life's Nebuchadnezzars and as Lord for all suffering Hebrew boys who dare to stand for a cause.

---

[2] "How Firm a Foundation."

Fear: The Enemy of Faith

Samuel D. Proctor

John 14:25-31

"Let not your heart be troubled, neither let it be afraid"
(John 14:27).

In order to understand what Jesus is talking about in the fourteenth chapter of John, we have to follow the conversation from chapters 12 and 13, for our text is the climax of a very dramatic series of events; it was spoken by Jesus after he had finished his last supper and a rather sudden shift in the atmosphere had occurred.

A few days earlier a crowd had strewn palm branches in the street and shouted, "Hosanna: Blessed is the King of Israel that cometh in the name of the Lord." But by the time of the supper, clouds of doubt and fear had gathered. All week long, since Palm Sunday, Jesus had astonished the disciples with his remarks about dying, about leaving, about being lifted up from the earth, and about being betrayed. They were dazed. They had left behind their farms, their families, their fishing boats and nets and tax-collecting jobs, and now it seemed that he would go, and they would be left in confusion and ridicule. Little wonder, then, that fear was written all over their faces and that confusion had spread among them. Their whole world was caving in on them.

At the close of the supper, the situation was no clearer to

them. Jesus had gone about washing their feet to signify his love for them and their bond of loyalty. He had so little time to be assured that they understood him and would carry on, and they were so bewildered that in verse 12 of the thirteenth chapter he went back to the table, sat down again, and went on to prepare them for his arrest and his execution. By then they knew beyond a doubt what was to happen, and they were brought low.

Simon Peter tried to show some strength. He told Jesus that he would die for him, but Jesus saw through that and told his chief disciple that he would not last through the night without denying him. Everything was falling apart; the seams were ripping fast.

Jesus took the time to help them with their disillusionment, their fear, and their obvious confusion. The fourteenth chapter of John is a source of comfort for countless believers, but it was given first to strengthen the trembling hearts of these eleven nervous disciples. What they needed was an elevation of their faith. Fear had moved in and taken over, and faith had to be revived. Life teaches us that *fear* is the enemy of *faith*, and the answer to fear is faith. Jesus tried to strengthen the disciples' faith, and he went as far as he could before he had to summarize the whole thing, "Let not your heart be troubled, neither let it be afraid."

Some of us would have been right at home among those disciples, because some of us live with fear and nervousness all the time. Even when there is no crisis, we conjure up one, get on the telephone and solicit one, put one together out of any rumor fragments that are passing around. "Elouise, did you hear what I heard? I suppose that means. . . ," and there it goes—something else to get upset about.

Of course, if you look hard enough there is always something to get frightened about: water being polluted with carcinogenic chemicals, the air clouded with nuclear dust, or South Africa blowing up one morning, unannounced. Then there is cancer randomly selecting its victims and drug abuse invading our families at unsuspecting times and street violence lurking always. There is always something to take your breath away if you look for it.

We'll never be able to prepare for the sheer chance of unpredictable, tragic events. A few years ago, in a quiet Southern community, a wonderful wife and mother was finishing dinner and casually reading her evening paper when a policeman fired a shot to stop a suspect running from a crime scene. The bullet struck a metal cleat on a power-line pole and ricocheted through her window, killing her instantly. She was the wife of one of Richmond, Virginia's leading physicians and the mother of a fine daughter.

How on earth can one prepare for that? Life cannot consist of our hiding in closets, crawling under beds, pulling the blankets over our heads, and sleeping with the television blasting. We can't walk every street sliding against the walls, peeping around every corner, and screaming every time a passerby puts hands in his or her pockets. Neither can you read the paper every morning waving spirits of ammonia under your nose! Something else must be the answer, and something else is.

You cannot give your heart to fear and waste your life. Jesus told his disciples that they would not be left alone. He promised them a Comforter, the prevailing, ever-present nearness of a loving and a caring God who has all power in his hands. And that promise is good for you and me and covers our condition. "Let not your heart be troubled, neither let it be afraid." Surely the economy *could* get worse, the warmongers *could* get something going, the poor *may* riot in the streets, Social Security *may* run out before we get ours, the creek *may* rise, Grandma *may* fall down the stairs, and the cows *may not* give any milk; but I can't keep my throat swollen, my knees shaking, and my breath short waiting for these awful things to come to pass. I have to face this day with my chin up, my shoulders back, my chest out, and my whole self going about my Father's business.

We cannot behave as though we had no Heavenly Father. We can't lay our religion down like that. "The LORD is my light and my salvation; whom shall I fear? the LORD is the strength of my life; of whom shall I be afraid?"

If all you have to count on is your quick wit, your own feeble strength, and the few facts available to your finite mind, you may have to go on living with your fear. But a believing child of God has more than that. "They that wait upon the LORD shall renew their strength; they shall mount up with wings as eagles; they shall run, and not be weary; and they shall walk, and not be faint."

However, one cannot talk about fear without having to admit

up front that, no matter whatever else we may say about it, legitimate fear is an important human emotion and one that we cannot live without. It is good to know when to be justifiably afraid. The Bible has a lot to say about the kind of arrogance that tempts God and the kind of fear that has its proper place in our lives. ". . . The fear of the Lord, that is wisdom; and to depart from evil is understanding" (Job 28:28).

The fear of God is the kind of fear that is a partner to faith. Indeed, life loses its bearing and we drift aimlessly when we arrogate to ourselves our own standard and set our own criteria as though there were no God at all. The psalmist said, "The fear of the LORD is the beginning of wisdom . . ." (Psalm 111:10). This is where our orientation to life starts, with an awareness that we did not create ourselves and that we are accountable to God. And we *should* feel estranged and fearful when we turn against God.

On the other hand, we must acknowledge that there is that neurotic kind of fear, that nagging uncertainty about everything and everybody that is quite different from the healthy kind of fear that turns on caution lights when they *ought* to be turned on. There are times when your heart should beat faster, when your adrenalin should start flowing, when your lips are supposed to get parched, and your throat ought to get dry. It is all appropriate and justifiable when real danger is approaching.

One afternoon, when we lived in Teaneck, our three-year-old managed to get into our station wagon when our attention was elsewhere. When we turned to find him, we discovered that he had left his tricycle and was all but hidden from view, sitting in our Ford station wagon at the steering wheel, with the brake released, the gear-shift lever in neutral, and the wagon rolling down the driveway into the busy street. He was yelling; we were screaming; everyone's color had changed, and our hearts were thumping. It was time for that kind of reaction!

When your junior-high-aged daughter comes home three nights in a row after 11 P.M. and you hear a strange car door click and the car leaves the scene screeching and there is no explanation for these anonymous rides home, you should get frightened! When your teenage son sleeps at every chance for hours on end, with no interest in sports, dancing, books, fishing, working, dressing, hiking, or playing music—just sleeping—it is time to be afraid. When your husband starts drinking alone every day, and going to bed intoxicated night after night, that's the time to be afraid. In fact, it's overdue!

How tragic it is when some really fine people are not alert to danger signals and incur serious problems of health, financial disaster, marital stress, and career chaos. And how purely "lucky" some of us are that some danger signs that we ran right through did not yield the consequences that they could have. In my college days a gang of friends and I would visit from campus to campus, participating in fraternity initiations. Now and then the initiation was followed by a banquet, and some of the young brothers "fellowshipped" heavily. One night, leaving Richmond after such a banquet, we begged the driver of our car to let someone else drive. He was stubborn and insisted that he could drive. Within minutes he had flipped us over three times in an old 1932 Chevrolet, built before the metal tops were used! We were saved only because there were nine of us tightly packed in a five-passenger car. Letting someone drive while intoxicated was a good time to be fearful, but we weren't; and we nearly died, all nine of us.

On a larger scale, when we see the Pentagon staffed so heavily with ex–gun merchants, when we see consultants for munitions firms turning up as Cabinet secretaries and assistant secretaries of the army, navy, air force or state, it is time to get scared. The alarms should wail. Peeping from under beds and hiding behind every door is one thing; but going through life with blinders on, oblivious to clear and present danger, is uncalled for. There is a place for legitimate fear, and we are equipped to react in very visible ways when we are genuinely afraid.

Looking further into this, legitimate fear is understandable, but chronic fear is a corrosive and destructive force. Chronic fear takes away all incentive, drains our initiative, kills our sense of adventure and saps creativity. Life does not give us many guarantees. The outcomes of most of our efforts are still big guesses. There are not many assurances available. Most of what we do is a risk, and you cannot live if fear is gnawing at you—fear of tall buildings, fear of bridges, fear of getting married, fear of asking for an overdue raise, fear of conversation with a new acquaintance, fear of people whose skin color, eye color, hair texture may be different, fear of a new book, fear of a new idea, fear of joining a new church.

Our faith approaches life in other terms altogether. The psalmist assures us: "The Lord is my shepherd, and I shall not want. . . . He leads me. . . . He restores my soul. . . . his rod and staff . . . comfort me. . . . my cup runs over. . . . goodness and mercy shall follow me. . . ." Life is a faith proposition. One must set certain faith hypotheses before each endeavor and then act, live, proceed, trust, and behave as though those hypotheses were true, and that very acting, living, proceeding, trusting, and behaving will make them true!

When I was nineteen years old, a shipfitter's apprentice in the naval shipyard at Norfolk, Virginia, I had a conviction that I was called to preach. I went to the labor board to resign my apprenticeship in order to return to college and to continue in a theological seminary. I shall never forget a man who stood in line behind me and who tried to persuade me not to seek further education for my calling. He told me of dozens of men who were preaching with no schooling at all and who seemed to be doing well. He thought I was foolish for giving up a "good job with a future." Nevertheless, without any assurances at all, without the usual guarantees, but with a faith suspended over an unknown future, and acting as though that future were assured—"the substance of things hoped for, the evidence of things not seen"—I left, returned to college, then went on to seminary and further study. The opportunities and challenges that life has afforded, through the providence of God, would never have been opened before me had I taken that stranger's advice. He tried to frighten me with predictions of possible failure, but my faith hypothesis proved sufficient. Without faith the journey is impossible, and fear is the enemy of faith.

Any serious task, any undertaking that really tests our commitment will require us to look beyond the incomplete data, beyond the fears that are so easily conjured and to make a leap based on a faith surmise.

Many years ago I was asked to take a trip with several other consultants into Israel, Syria, Lebanon, Jordan, Pakistan, India, and Burma. I had never been to these places. World War II had just ended, and these nations were largely in an unsettled state. The purpose of the mission was to work out transfers of American-owned schools, colleges, and hospitals to the newly independent, indigenous peoples. It was a de-Americanization program, timely and urgent. I was told all sorts of things to make me dizzy, to make my knees shake, to dry my mouth, to make my stomach quiver. But words from the heart of an ancient Bedouin child of God kept flooding my mind: "God is our refuge and strength, a very present help in trouble. Therefore will not we fear, though the earth be removed, and though the mountains be carried into the midst of the sea . . ." (Psalm 46:1-2).

Of course, such faith ought never to fly in the face of hard, cold facts. Faith begins where the facts leave off; but the facts are hard to get at in most areas of life, and we are compelled to walk by an enlightened faith. It is sheer ignorance to try to *substitute* faith for hard facts, and we don't need to. There are plenty of other uses for faith! When all *available* facts are in, life still requires faith! If you are trying to judge the wisdom of getting married, the *facts* go only so far; after that it is *faith*! And, without faith—hard, solid, steady, warm, vibrant faith— one should forget it.

The amazing thing is that faith is quite available and inexpensive—cheaper than alcohol, cocaine, and all of the narcotics and barbiturates to which fear drives us. Think of it. Without such artificial stimuli, those uneducated, impoverished followers of Jesus walked out to face Roman procurators, Syrian kings, and hostile crowds in town after town, spreading the gospel of the Son of God. And in three short centuries Christianity became the official religion of the same empire that Pontius Pilate had represented. The cross was raised above the Roman eagle. And it all began that scary night when Jesus saw fear in all of the disciples' faces and said to them, "Let not your heart be troubled, neither let it be afraid" (John 14:27).

So in the end this admonition divides us into two camps, really: on the one hand, there are those who can be comfortable only with the safest propositions. And on the other are those who know when to be afraid but who refuse to let fear ground them. They have learned that fear is the enemy of faith. Here we are in a world where whole continents were found by adventurers who knew the proper place of fear but who put faith ahead of it. We enjoy freedom of the press, freedom of religion, freedom of assembly, and a democratic form of government by virtue of those who gave fear its place but put faith in front of it!

And if we are ever going to have a world without war, a

society without racial hatred, and an economy that gives every-one a chance to earn the necessities and comforts of life, we must realize that they will not come by the weak resolution of frightened leaders, searching for the safest place to stand. They will come because of leaders with faith, whose eyes can behold the distant vistas of a better day and then align their actions behind such a vision.

Recently on a flight from Oslo to Stockholm where I was to attend a conference, I was fortunate enough to be seated beside a professional interpreter, who had been born in Russia, been reared in Sweden, lived in America for a brief while, and was now working as an international translator. She said that when she visits Russia she hears the people there wonder why America is planning to destroy Russia; and when she visits America she hears the people here wonder why Russia is planning to destroy America! She told of a Russian mother weeping bitterly because her son was drafted to serve in the Russian occupation of Afghanistan. And she said that earlier in America she saw a mother weep the same way when her son was drafted to go to Vietnam. This madness goes on and on.

The answers to all of this lie beyond our pettiness and fear, but they will call for women and men of faith to take those rare and novel initiatives to lead us to those answers. Our own society was burdened for years with the awful contradiction of *apartheid* in a Christian society. There were big brick churches on every downtown street, singing those great Wesley lines:

> A charge to keep I have,
> A God to glorify;
> A never-dying soul to save,
> And fit it for the sky.[1]

And while the white Christians were singing those lines, the blacks were across town at the same hour singing:

> Arm me with jealous care,
> As in thy sight to live,
> And O thy servant, Lord, prepare,
> A strict account to give![2]

[1] "A Charge to Keep I Have."
[2] *Ibid.*

It appeared that this arrangement of separate worship was ordained by God to last always. Everyone had become accustomed to it. It seemed that only a miracle could change it. Fear of change had frozen the entire situation. Some of life's greatest opportunities are lost to the phantom of unwarranted fear. But God raised up leaders like Martin Luther King, Jr., whose faith left no room for fear, and a change came over the South. It is not the same as it used to be; those fears turned out to be ghosts.

Those scared disciples thought that Pilate and Caiaphas had won, that Jesus would be wiped out, that they would be scattered to hide like wanted felons. But Jesus looked into those frightened faces and said, "Let not your heart be troubled, neither let it be afraid." He called them out of their preoccupation with their safety and security and invited them to lean on the everlasting arms of God.

You see, conventional wisdom says, "Play it safe. Don't take any chances." But a wisdom beyond our own says, "Trust in the LORD with all thine heart; and lean not unto thine own understanding" (Proverbs 3:5). The voice of fear says, "Self-preservation is the first law of nature," but the voice of faith says, "Seek ye first the kingdom of God, and his righteousness; and all these things shall be added unto you" (Matthew 6:33). The voice of fear says, "Don't start what you can't finish," but the voice of faith says, ". . . Be not afraid, neither be thou dismayed: for the LORD thy God is with thee whithersoever thou goest!" (Joshua 1:9).

"Let not your heart be troubled, neither let it be afraid."

On Giving Up on People Too Soon

Samuel D. Proctor

Acts 15:39-40; 2 Timothy 4:11

". . . And so Barnabas took Mark. . . . And Paul chose Silas . . ." (Acts 15:39-40). "Take Mark, and bring him with thee: for he is profitable to me . . ." (2 Timothy 4:11).

No one is going to live this life without some failures. It simply does not happen that one goes from one stage of life to the next, facing the temptations, the uncertainties, the obstacles and adversities that we all face, without stumbling and falling somewhere along the road. Life is made up of conditions and circumstances over which we do not have complete control. Even when one has done the very best that one can, when one has guarded against all error and prepared for every contingency, then the unforeseen, the unexpected, the unpredictable will happen, and one will taste the bitter dregs of defeat and failure that lie at the bottom of everyone's cup of life.

The Bible is so wonderful because it does not leave out any aspect of human experience. Just as an artist, painting the picture of a human face, will capture the beauty and the symmetry of that face and will also faithfully copy the moles, the wrinkles, the tiny scars, and the reflection of the wear of the years in the corners around the eyes, so the Bible tells it like it really is. One portion of the Bible tells of a fine young man, John Mark, who began life with great promise but failed early.

In Acts 15 we read of the glowing success that Paul and Barnabas had on their first missionary journey. They had preached Christ in strange places, and the power of the Holy Spirit had followed them. They had planted churches in strategic places and had opened up the world for the advance of the faith. Paul and Barnabas had carried with them a young man named John Mark. In fact, he was the nephew of Barnabas, his sister Mary's son.

But Mark failed. In fact, he did not even finish the journey. The men were on the first leg, preaching in the place where Mark's mother was born and raised, when Mark quit, packed up, and went home to Jerusalem and to his mother Mary. We do not know why he quit. Maybe he was too young. Maybe it was too frightening traveling by foot from one hostile town to another. Maybe he was hungry and thirsty. Maybe he became homesick or had stomach trouble or couldn't stand Paul's disposition or lost interest or just missed his friends back in Jerusalem. Whatever the reason, Paul didn't like it, and when Mark wanted to go on the second journey, Paul said, "No!"

This must have been embarrassing because Mark's uncle, Barnabas, was a leader in the first church in Jerusalem. He was a man of some standing. When Paul was converted on the Damascus road and nobody at headquarters believed it, Barnabas was the one man who presented Paul to the church at Jerusalem. Barnabas was *somebody*. The first church in Jerusalem had a branch in Antioch, and Barnabas was the chief preacher. He led that church for a year. He was there when the word "Christian" was first used. Pastor Barnabas was the man in charge.

When a famine swept through the Holy Land and the people in Jerusalem were without food, it was Barnabas who brought money down from Antioch to feed Peter, James, John, the brothers of Jesus, and the other believers. Barnabas was somebody special.

And Mary, his sister, was somebody, too. Remember, it was at her house that the meetings were held when the church was just starting. When Peter came out of jail for preaching, he had nowhere else to go except to the home of John Mark and Mary, headquarters for the church. Mark had a strong mother and a very highly respected and faithful uncle named Barnabas.

So, here is Mark. A young failure in life. And things could go either way with him. Would a young life be wasted? Would a career be ruined? Could he turn this failure into success? Should Paul give up on Mark? Did Mark deserve a second chance? Was Paul too hard on him? Don't we sometimes give up on people too soon? Aren't there too many persons whose lives have been unfulfilled because someone gave up on them too soon?

Of course, all of this says something about Paul also. He could lose his temper, and he was not that easy to cope with. Ask Simon Peter; he could surely tell you! From what we know about Paul, it is not surprising that some of these young men gave up on him.

We can only imagine what travel was like in those days. Maybe the food was bad, for example. Maybe there were too many mosquitoes for tent dwelling, and perhaps Paul was moving too fast. He must have had boundless energy. Without any kind of public transportation or the conveniences that we take for granted today—hot running water, rest rooms, and so on—he pressed on from one continent to another, one national capital after another, and traveled on rough seas without the kind of navigational facilities we have today. He was always living dangerously, hiking through dark mountain passes and sultry deserts. This was Paul's territory.

It had to be tough on a young man to leave home and go out with Paul where it was hard to find fresh food, clean water, and a comfortable place to sleep. Then, with all of that, Mark was dealing with a man who did not mind going to jail every now and then! There need not be a mystery about why John Mark would be tempted to give up and go on back home.

Yet John Mark came back. What a mistake Paul would have made, giving up on John Mark too soon!

It would be wonderful to have all the details of what happened from the day that Paul fired John Mark to those lonely days that Paul spent in a Roman prison with John Mark at his side. In his letter to Timothy, Paul writes, "Only Luke is with me. Take Mark, and bring him with thee: for he is profitable to me for the ministry." And to the Colossians he writes of those who are standing by him faithfully and he mentions one Aristarchus, a fellow prisoner, and on the next breath he speaks of John Mark, nephew of Barnabas. What a mistake

Paul would have made, giving up on John Mark too soon!

Reflecting on John Mark's behavior, we are reminded that young folk are in a growth process, experimenting with life, and sometimes we may be tempted to give up on them too soon. Those of us who are parents must understand this. A little reflection on our own lives also will remind us that it is not that easy! In order for young people to ripen and mature, they're going to make mistakes. John Mark faced no ordinary moral challenge. He had a great deal expected of him. He had a chance to make a mistake. He "blew" an opportunity and "blew" it badly.

Come and see that fortunately this first big blunder in life is often a temporary setback. Isn't it wonderful that most people we know lose ground for just a little while and then they make a comeback like John Mark! They find their way back sooner or later. Of course, it's always disappointing to see a beautiful life lose its footing. Tragically, this is often associated with an unsuccessful marriage or some kind of crisis in one's work. It is often the outcome of a long and clumsy wrestling with Satan and experimenting with some of life's worst moral tangents.

I'll never forget a visit I had from a very prominent citizen when I was an administrator with the Peace Corps. He said to me with one eye squinting, "You don't know me, but I know about you." He went on, without hesitation, and, in a trembling voice, he said, "I've been casting around the country trying to find a place where my young pastor can make a new start." He said someone had told him that if there was any place in the nation where people would be sympathetic and listen, it might be the Peace Corps. The Corps might help the pastor and get him on an assignment far out of the country to make a new beginning.

He said, "I love my pastor. He has spent fifteen beautiful years with us. Recently he got into sensitivity training. He began the 'touch and feel stuff.' You know pastors are under such pressure: they have to keep thinking up new things, and sometimes they go overboard with new ideas before they really understand them thoroughly. He got into this psychological 'bag,' you know, and he was training folks about how to get closer to one another. He was listening to a lot of people's secrets. Some women were freely telling about their infidelities. Young girls were telling about affairs they had had with persons of high position in town. He began to find out that a great many Christians had been 'tipping out' and having fun.

"And he said to me that in a moment of weakness he just thought he'd been missing something. Then he went on into a more serious part; he said that as he began helping these people with their problems and facing their moral dilemmas, the next thing he knew he was involved with *one* of them himself, and later with *another*."

He said, "Brother Proctor, I'm telling you about a fine, God-called preacher who is in deep trouble."

He said, "I've left my work, left my desk piled up, and I'm roaming around the country trying to find a way to lift this young man out of that situation and get him a long way off so that he can get a new grip on life."

He said, "If you could find a spot somewhere in Asia, in Africa, in South America, anywhere! Get him away from where he is right now."

Bad as this situation was, and as hopeless as it appeared, here was a friend with the love of God in his heart who did not want to give up on that young man too soon!

Some of us are in unhappy situations at work; some have problems with money; and some drown ourselves in all kinds of rationalizations, and we do lose our discipline. We face these moral dilemmas, and the strength to fight the Tempter we simply can't find anymore.

> Where is that blessedness I knew
> When first I saw the Lord?
> Where is the soul-refreshing view
> Of Jesus and his word?
> Return, O holy Dove, return,
> Sweet messenger of rest!
> I hate the sins that made thee mourn
> And drove thee from my breast.[1]

Next, however, we must allow for the fact that some Christians simply never did become converted sufficiently. They loved the idea of being in church. They quoted Scriptures and took Communion but never did understand the compassion of God and the love of Christ.

I have found some who lie and speak ugly to folk all the time. I know some who hate the poor, hate the weak, hate the

[1] "O for a Closer Walk with God."

sick, hate unpopular people, and are always seeking the friendship of "up-front" and successful persons. They brag about the "winners" they have in their circle and make clear the fact that they have no time for the "losers." And the Christ they profess spent all of his earthly days *with* the "losers" and those *farthest from* the inner circle! The kind of folk that Jesus associated with all the time are not their kind of people. They are striving to be *recognized, rewarded, honored, seen,* and *glorified!* Sick egotism all around us!

They dearly love the present world! They have given up on all of the things of the Spirit. They've got to have something new and dazzling all the time. The strobe lights have got to be flashing around them constantly. They are never satisfied with what they have. They are always looking for novelties, something bright with no space between delights—thrill seeking all the time! No time for reflection about life and death, joy and sorrow, sin and forgiveness, God and his greatness, or the search for the good, the beautiful, the true, and the ultimate. None of these things appeals any longer, so they go back to "the present world" and are strong candidates for severe losses.

Finally, as a preacher of this marvelous gospel, I must affirm that God in Christ does not give up on us, not ever. The John Marks of the world are under his watchful eye. If you know anyone who has a lapse like that, if you have a lapse like that in your own life, I want you to know that some of the finest names in the whole religious history that lies behind us had lapses too. Paul talked about how he had gone off the deep end, how he ran off and persecuted Christians. He could never forget standing there, watching people stone Stephen, and hearing Stephen say, "Father, forgive them. Lay not this sin to their charge." He was haunted by it, and whenever he was in deep trouble, he was happy to say, "I saw a light brighter than the noonday sun!"

So many souls have walked in the brightness of God's morning of forgiveness only after lurking in the darkness of the ugliest sins. Simon Peter led the young church, but look at how far he had to come. Jesus looked at him at that Last Supper and said, "Simon, Satan wants to sift you like wheat." Before morning Simon had lied and said he never knew Jesus.

So this is not new to us who preach. We've seen an awful lot of John Marks in our present time. And this gives us our greatest opportunity to see to it that that lapse is not a long one or a permanent one but a brief one and that restoration is made.

This is what makes preaching so wonderful and so challenging. There are a great many John Marks out there who have not come back yet, who are wallowing in the mire of their mistakes. Nobody knows exactly what happened to them. Today it's so easy for one to get lost. The temptations are everywhere. We're drowning in pornography. The home now is permeated with TV filth. Filth! They have the audacity to call them *adult* movies. It's awful when one has to qualify a movie by saying it's filthy enough now so that it's ready for adult use! What must children be thinking of "adult" tastes and requirements!

The moral standards that we learned to live by have been erased, one right after another. This is a terrible time for someone to be trying to live a life of discipline in the Spirit. Our children have so few examples to follow. They hear of important leaders lying, those in public life taking bribes, and all kinds of moral failure occurring in high places. Urban life itself allows for a certain mischievous privacy and anonymity. Grandma isn't there watching. That big, old oak tree that would speak to you if it could talk isn't there. That old backyard swing you haven't seen for a long time. Everybody we see is a stranger. This means that one is left purely on his or her own. What an awful circumstance in which to try to avoid moral collapse! Many have found it to be absolutely too much to handle.

I boarded a taxi not long ago in New York City as I headed for an engagement, and the driver said, "You look like you're in a hurry, fella." I said, "Yes, I've got to get to a church in a very few minutes." He said, "I'll see what I can do to help you."

By then he had gotten a glimpse of my face. He said, "Are you from Norfolk?" "Yes." "You went to Booker Washington high school?" "Yes." "What class were you in?" "Class of '37." "Uh-huh," he mumbled. "You have a sister? Four brothers?" "Yes." Then there was silence.

I said slowly, "Well, you must know me. Who are you?" "Well," he said, "I was in Norfolk around that time." He didn't say much after that.

When I got out to pay him, he held back his hand. "Don't

pay me, DeWitt." He used my middle name! He knew me well. He then put the light on. He took off his hat as if to show some respect or to make a gesture of approval. I saw his face clearly. He *was* from our town. Then he was so handsome and clean-cut, so popular, so aspiring; but when I saw him, his eyes were bloodshot with big dark bags beneath them, and there were deep crevices in his face, marks of a rough existence.

Getting out, I leaned back into the window, and I said without thinking, "What, in the name of God, has happened to you in New York?" He put his car in gear, shut the door fast, put out the light, and sped away.

When I asked his friends later what had happened to him in New York, they said that he went up there and sank so low so fast and stayed there so long that he simply fell apart. The "world" had a hold on him.

When I see that and go into church and start preaching, I ask God to give me the right words to say and to tell me the right songs to sing and to give me the skill in preaching that can stir somebody's heart, because I know that there is a John Mark there trying to find his way back from an awful failure.

I remember so well, as a college freshman in Virginia, high above the Appomatox River "on a lofty hill," I was trying hard to escape and to deny my rearing. I was fast forgetting Grandma and Daddy and Mamma and the Bank Street Baptist Church. I was with other freshmen trying to explore everything that the devil held before us. Then I would go to the chapel, and too often there was someone *blushing* to speak to His name, someone afraid to talk about God in bold terms and who left me sunk down in my seat unmoved. And I was drifting farther and farther away.

But the Hound of Heaven, with unhurried pace found me through this labyrinthine way. One Sunday morning—I can remember it as though it were yesterday—I got up, and I said, "I'm going to sneak off this campus. I'm going to slide down this hill and find me a church!" I didn't know which one to go to, but God sent me to the Mount Zion Baptist Church where there was a preacher who wasn't playing and who wasn't trying to talk "smart" talk.

He took a text, and he said, "As I was with Moses so I will be with thee. I will neither fail thee nor forsake thee." Then he hit me right between my eyes. He said, "Therefore, be *strong* and of *good courage*. Be not afraid; neither be dismayed, for the Lord thy God is with thee withersoever thou goest." And he made me some strong promises in that sermon about God's unfailing love. He gave me a deal that I could not turn down.

I came out of my little seat and rushed on up there and thanked God that I believed once again that he would not fail me nor forsake me. And I kept going in the same direction from that morning on.

I didn't know what woke me up that morning. I didn't know who sent me to the Mount Zion Baptist Church. All I knew was that an angel of God must have told that preacher that I was there, a tall, skinny college freshman, drifting away from his moorings. And his words found a place in my longing heart and turned me around. Praise God!

What a privilege to know that John Mark somehow covered the distance between the day Paul fired him and that day at Rome with Paul and Peter when he wrote the first Gospel. What a good thing that Paul did not give up on him too soon!

The Bottom Line

Samuel D. Proctor

Matthew 25:31-46

In Matthew 25:31-46 Jesus is summarizing what he has been teaching and preaching for three years. The time is getting short. The Cross is two days away, and he does not have much opportunity left to make things any plainer to his followers. As he often did, he folded it all up in one vivid, succinct, unambiguous parable that a child could understand.

He said that when the Son of man comes to judge the nations, he will separate them like a shepherd divides the sheep from the goats. And he would say to the sheep on his right hand, ". . . I was an hungred, and ye gave me meat: I was thirsty, and ye gave me drink: I was a stranger, and ye took me in: Naked and ye clothed me: I was sick, and ye visited me: I was in prison, and ye came unto me." And the sheep will ask when had they seem him hungry, or thirsty, or a stranger, or naked, or sick or in prison. "And the King shall answer and say unto them, Verily I say unto you, Inasmuch as ye have done it unto one of the least of these my brethren, ye have done it unto me."

Then he will say to the goats on his left that he was hungry and they gave him no meat, thirsty and they gave him no drink, a stranger and they would not take him in, naked and they did not clothe him, sick and in prison and they would not visit him. And the goats will ask when they had seen him hungry, thirsty, a stranger, naked, sick in prison. And he will reply, "Inasmuch as ye did not to one of the least of these, ye did it not to me." And he will send them away "into everlasting punishment: but the righteous into life eternal."

It is embarrassing to see how straightforward Jesus was in setting out the basic requirements of God for his people and how confusing and complicated we have made it. We have seen Europe soaked in blood over religious wars, fighting for thirty years at a time, a hundred years, burning scholars on the stake, beheading so-called heretics, imprisoning Bible translators, and driving millions of people to exile. And yet Jesus, in simple clarity, gave us the bottom line: "I was an hungred and ye gave me meat; I was thirsty, and ye gave me drink: I was a stranger, and ye took me in: Naked, and ye clothed me: I was sick, and ye visited me: I was in prison, and ye came unto me." That's the very bottom line.

We have written millions of books about Jesus. We have fought over how much water we need in order to baptize in his name. We have broken up churches on how to remember him with simple bread and wine and created two hundred fifty religious denominations in the United States alone, in his name.

I recall taking a church history examination in seminary on which I was asked to explain the difference between *consubstantiation* and *transubstantiation*, between *homo-ousios* and *homoi-ousios*. One question asked me to describe *antidisestablishmentarianism*! And Jesus said, "I was hungry and you gave me meat." *That* is the bottom line. If the Master saw those examination questions, he would never have believed that they had anything to do with himself! But Christians, for centuries, with long, serious faces, wearing heavy gowns, and shut away from the real world, have spent their lives on such questions.

One of the obvious problems here is that most of us are not close enough to the hungry, the thirsty, the naked, the stranger, the sick or the prison bound. Our life's chances were so much better than theirs that we have outdistanced them and we don't even know their names and addresses. We have no one-on-one access to these "losers" in our society. And, as a matter of fact, some of us are not that sure about our own station in life, and we don't want to get too close to "the least of these" and risk being taken for one of them!

Recently, I asked a leading Christian minister from India what changes had taken place in the condition of the "untouchables," the outcastes, those who live beneath the lowest caste in Hindu society, in the last twenty years. He replied that he had not noticed any change, except that they had migrated into the cities in larger numbers and that they were protesting more vigorously against their economic plight.

But he did not stop there. He said that they had no advocates, even though 90 percent of India's nineteen million Christians came from the untouchables themselves. Those Christians have out-distanced "the least of these." Yet, Jesus said that in the final judgment the sheep will be those who have fed the hungry, given drink to the thirsty, clothed the naked, taken in the stranger, and visited the sick and the prison bound. Our priorities notwithstanding, this *is* the bottom line.

It is true, however, that it could get to be rather clumsy if all of us tried to volunteer to take care of the world's neediest on a purely spontaneous, personal, charitable basis. A curious suggestion was made recently by the mayor of New York City when asking churches to take care of New York's homeless victims. This is clearly a task that ought not be shoved off on the uneven and unreliable, spontaneous goodwill of a few people of modest means while a million others shrug it off. Obviously, it was not a serious suggestion. Yet President Reagan has given hints that the churches should divide the poor families among them; again, a suggestion that had to be purely impromptu, for the number of poor families left would remain a staggering problem.

We are too far from the early frontier days for such small-scale, primitive, responses to national needs. It is almost like asking every family to install its own water purification plant and to vaccinate its own children. Reverting to such private efforts, without "big" government programs, we would run the risk of having smallpox and diptheria return. Some would even give up public schools and risk massive ignorance as a national experiment!

No. Our care of the hungry, the thirsty, the naked, and the prison bound is still largely a public obligation; but we are not finished when we say that. The obligation requires caring Christians to stay on the case, to participate in the political arena, to be involved in public policy making so that *we all* don't end up as "goats" on the left hand of the righteous judge.

Some things that we have heard recently from high places tell us that not everyone agrees that the hungry *should* be fed or that the naked *should* be clothed. Some people are more interested in blaming the victims, holding them responsible for their own condition. A gross ignorance is abroad in the land on how the poor became poor, on how deeply entrenched job discrimination has been, on how inadequate some education has been, and on how much hatred and rank hostility many people have had to endure while trying to hold on to a little dignity.

How easy it is for those who have arrived to forget! And, not many have earned the good fortune that they inherited. I once heard an old preacher say, "If you ever see a turtle on a tree stump, you know it didn't get there by itself!" Too many of us are turtles on tree stumps who forgot how we got there!

We have not begun to examine our institutions closely enough with that objective, cool, intense, long-term persistence of which we are so capable or to find a way to offer everyone an ample opportunity to overcome marginal existence.

Yet, having acknowledged the problems of a one-on-one response to "the least of these"—a purely voluntary, spontaneous outpouring of goodwill—it is true that more often than we care to recall, we have stood face to face with a need and with a clear, unambiguous chance to do something that would make a difference, and we have rationalized our way around it.

One day when I was a young college president, a student came by to tell me that his money had run out and that he had to leave school. In those days presidents knew students by name and knew much about their personal circumstances. But this student gave me some details about himself that I had not known. He said that he was a "country orphan." That is a child who gets passed around from one willing family to another with no legal papers signed by anyone. The last family to have him had died, and he needed to get out and "regroup." His immediate need was for someone to drive him some fifty miles into the country to get an old trunk and some fragments of furniture and household items that he cherished and thought he needed.

My first response was to brush it off, officially, as something beyond my office and let luck take care of his need. I tried that, and I even told myself that it was beneath a college president to take a school van or truck and drive a country orphan fifty miles into the woods to pick up scraps of junk. I had *almost* sold myself on that idea except for *one* thing: I had read too much, sung too much, prayed too long, and preached too often,

> Take my life and let it be
> Consecrated, Lord, to thee;
> Take my hands, and let them move
> At the impulse of thy love. . . .
>
> Take my will and make it Thine;
> It shall be no longer mine;
> Take my heart, it is thine own!
> It shall be Thy royal throne. . . .[1]

The next thing I knew, I had gotten the school's pickup truck, changed my clothes, and the student and I had headed out for the country to get a country orphan's leavings. And the trip went fast because we sang and talked about the life of a country orphan all the way. That old truck seemed like the upper room where the Spirit descended or the temple where Isaiah saw the Lord. It was a benchmark for me, and brief moments like that have been spread over my years, and they have blessed me.

"Lord, when saw we thee a stranger, or naked, or hungry. . . ." "Inasmuch as ye did it to the least of these my brethren, ye did it unto me." The bottom line.

One other problem is that we allow no room, no space, no time in our lives for this kind of activity, this concern. "Our programs are crowded, and we are in a big hurry, Jesus. We understand *you*, but you don't understand *us*! We live in the real world," we protest, "and this simple idealism has no place here." We are caught up in an urbanized, technological culture that is marked by competitiveness, and we are taught to be predatory, greedy, cunning, and ambitious. The side effect is that we have become hedonists, devoted to our personal delights, and narcissistic, lovers of ourselves before everyone else. It is a new idolatry, self-worship! So we have no time for the "least of these."

[1] "Take My Life, and Let It Be."

This creeps into our institutions, and we forget why they exist. A very large church in one of our major cities was sending over $100,000 a year to Nigeria to convert and educate Yorubas in the Christian faith. Many Nigerians benefited from this generous effort; several achieved doctor's degrees in some of America's finest universities. But one Sunday morning a small group of Nigerians appeared and sought to worship in that magnificent church. And officers of the church, prominent businessmen, fraternal leaders, and persons of high standing in town, stood on the marble steps of that massive colonial building and denied those young Yorubas, with tribal marks on their cheeks and with an education provided by funds from that *very* church, *denied* them a chance to worship in the name of the One who said, ". . . I was a stranger and ye took me not in."

One wonders what was said around the Lord's table when the decision was made to do such a thing, even in the 1950s. How did this action relate to the Christ whose praises the church members sang with such zest? Of course, many Christians have a strange view of their religion; they think that it only prepares them for death and heaven and that concern for the hungry, the hurt, the dispossessed, the alienated is some kind of liberalism or social gospel. By giving it such a label, they think they have gotten rid of the concern. But it was no "liberal" or "social gospel" propagandist who said, "Inasmuch as you did it not unto the least of these, ye did it not to me . . . . go away into everlasting punishment."

It appears that one sure way to go to hell is to ignore the so-called "social gospel"! The gospel, by its very nature, is social. If persons suffer in groups, that is "social." If groups *cause* the suffering, that makes it "social" also. "Social" refers only to how many persons are affected, and "the least of these my brethren" is more than one, single person. It is a cheap cop-out to use loaded labels in dealing with human suffering. If we are not prepared for discipleship, we should confess our weakness and ask for God's help. It is insincere to pretend that we do not understand what Jesus meant.

Clarence Jordan, the late director of the experimental farm called *Koinonia* in Americus, Georgia, was one of the finest preachers of the claims of Christ that we have had in our country. Once he was preaching to ministers at a Baptist conference in Green Lake, Wisconsin, when a preacher asked him straightforwardly, "Dr. Jordan, how can a modern, urban pastor preach the Sermon on the Mount and be a success?" Jordan replied, "Jesus did not give the Sermon on the Mount to successful, modern, urban pastors. He gave it to his disciples. You have to choose which you want to be if there is a conflict." This is the bottom line.

Thank God, every now and then we find a witness who helps us to understand what Jesus meant when he said, "I was a stranger and you took me in." Ed Tuller and his late wife, Rose, had a fine ministry at the American Church in Paris. One Sunday morning, they noticed a black child in church, a member of a refugee family from Uganda, with massive cataracts practically blinding both eyes. The Lord laid this on their hearts, and within weeks it happened that a worldwide ophthalmology conference on eye diseases, was held in Paris. When they spoke of this child's ailment, they found that a Jewish specialist, who lived near them back in New Jersey, and who attended that conference, volunteered to help the little girl to get surgery in New York. Rose and Ed spent an entire leave period shuttling back and forth between New Jersey and New York and attending to the needs of the Ugandan child whom they met in Paris. Later, a Hispanic surgeon operated and saved her sight in one eye. White Protestants, a New Jersey Jew, a Latin American, and a little girl from Uganda were caught up in living out what the Master meant when he said, "I was a stranger and ye took me in." The bottom line.

It is not too late for Christians to reclaim the power and authority of the Good News. God revealed to us in Christ his love and his expectation for the human family. He used a human life, a person with human dimensions like our own. Following him, we find the power, the authority, and the right to become the children of God. No one of us may ever do this to perfection, but by the grace of God, this is the direction in which we should be headed. This is the road we should be travelling; this is how life takes on joy and purpose. "I was hungry and you gave me meat. . . . I was a stranger and you took me in."

Finally, it gets clearer all the time how far God went to reach us. Even though God revealed himself to us in nature, in history, in logic, in music, and in mathematics, ultimately he deliberately chose the son of a poor, Galilean carpenter's family. God passed over the mighty and the powerful and came to us in a life close to the heartache, the pain, and the estrangement in the world; a life lived in an occupied land, among people living in a police state, under a cold, indifferent expatriate governor and a puppet king; a life begun in a barn in Bethlehem. Everywhere a person turned, there was somebody in trouble. And this was the point at which the God of wisdom and love chose to enter time out of eternity, in the very midst of the human struggle.

In the third chapter of Luke is a clue to God's purpose, which has been marvelously illuminated in a recorded sermon by Gardner C. Taylor. Luke is telling us who the important people were when Jesus was born: Tiberius was emperor; Pilate was governor; Herod was king, a tetrarch, ruler over one fourth of the realm; Phillip was a tetrarch; and Lysanias was still another tetrarch; Annas was a high priest, and so was Caiaphas. But the word of God came to *John*—and not to any of the above!—the son of Zacharias, in the wilderness. He had no title at all. He wore a loin cloth and ate locusts and honey. And the *Word* passed over all of those titled subjects and came to *John*; it passed by the palaces and the "most holy" places and found *John* in the wilderness. This almost says to us that if we really want to find God, we have to look for him somewhere other than around wealth and power, for somehow these thrive best where God is *not*, where God is excluded.

Preaching and witnessing for Christ will always be timeless and relevant, for each new generation has to be told the message again and again, in its own language and idiom. No one can inherit this message. The experience of finding God is more precious than finding a career, a spouse, or a lifetime job, for these things are all burdens without God. Yet isn't it strange how we tend to be naturally attracted to evil, rather than to God?

In my boyhood in Huntersville, a dusty hollow of Norfolk in those days, we had a familiar sight in our streets, a woman whose mind was defective and who pushed a cart constantly, picking up crepe paper, medicine bottles, coat hangers, broken toys, and you-name-it. She wore whatever she felt like wearing, winter clothes in hot summer weather, an evening gown that someone had thrown away, an abandoned fur coat—anything.

And the boys and girls, who had the nerve, would holler at her calling her "Crazy Ida!" Sometimes she would chase them or throw a bottle or a stick at them. Funny, I wanted to call her Crazy Ida too, but I couldn't find the nerve to do it.

Well, one day she rolled her cart slowly toward my end of the street, and I was alone, I thought. I checked all around to be sure, and then took my place in the lane beside our house, behind a bush. And just as she passed, I took in a deep breath and let the devil use me. "Crazy Ida," I shouted and ran like a thief.

But before I could get out of the back end of the lane, my mother had opened a side window that we never used. I could have dug a hole and crawled in. One gets embarrassed like that only two or three times in a full life span. She said, "Did you call her Crazy Ida?"

No reply. Just plain humiliation and shame. I had learned enough about Jesus to know better than to do what I did, but that awful, primordial, atavistic drag! Sin! It was so tempting to heap more pain on one already wounded deeply.

"Crazy Ida," Mamma said softly, which was not her style. "Don't call her that. She hasn't always been like she is today. We were girls together. She used to sing in choruses and recite poems like the rest of us, but she had a terrible marriage, and she broke under the strain. They took her children from her and sent her away. When she came back, her mind was gone. Don't add to her suffering."

She said more, but the impression has lasted for more than fifty years! I was so wrong. This is the bottom line: "Inasmuch as you did it to the least of these, you did it to me," Jesus said.

Good religion meets life right where it is and deals with it. And I fear that the Christian faith will have to get closer to the real issues of life before it can become relevant to these times. I see a generation out there, raised on television violence, who do not know Martin Luther King, Adam Clayton Powell, John F. Kennedy, or Rosa Parks except by reputation, who have only heard of the great depression, and who have not had to work for their spending money. Our generation has been preoccupied with alcohol, divorce, materialism, military expansion, racism, pornography, and making money. So no wonder this generation finds it hard to believe in God!

But if *we* followed Jesus more closely, the people of this

generation would see God in the Christ *we* serve and love. If *we* would lift him up in our own lives, they would say like the Greek visitors to the disciples, "Sir, we would see Jesus." They haven't met anyone like Jesus. They have not confronted any personality so compelling as Christ. They had not had their hearts touched like Jesus can touch them. They have not loved like Jesus can teach them to love. Their lives have never been changed like Jesus will change them, and nobody can take their talent, their strength, their fine abilities and harness them for good like Jesus can. Nobody can satisfy their curiosity, satiate their hunger, quench their thirst or revive their souls like Jesus can.

We used to sing in church,

> I heard the voice of Jesus say,
> "Behold I freely give
> The living water; thirsty one,
> Stoop down and drink, and live."[2]

People don't need to get high. They don't need to shoot up. They don't need to sniff coke, smoke pot, or pop pills. They don't need to drink themselves into oblivion or soak their brains with one chemical after another. All they need is to open their hearts to Christ!

> I came to Jesus, and I drank
> Of that life-giving stream;
> My thirst was quenched, my soul revived,
> And now I live in him.[3]

I'll never forget the image of Jesus that intrigued my mind so much so that I could not turn down his claim on my life. In Matthew 26:6 it is about halfway between Palm Sunday and Good Friday, Wednesday, and Jesus is in Bethany, at the house of Simon the Leper, having dinner. In Matthew 21:17 we read, "And he left them, and went out of the city into Bethany; and he lodged there." He took a room in Bethany on Palm Sunday night, and Wednesday he was still in Bethany at Simon's house. Of all the places for Jesus to be staying this last week on earth, the week before Calvary! He was lodging with a leper, a man with deep pits in his face, joints missing from his fingers and

---

[2] "I Heard the Voice of Jesus Say."
[3] *Ibid.*

toes, a man who was too much of an embarrassment, too unclean, to be allowed to live with his family or friends. (The entire thirteenth and fourteenth chapters of Leviticus explain how a leper is to be handled from the time the disease is found until he is declared cleansed. It is one long round of humiliation, ostracism, and separation from everybody!) And people must have asked Simon, "Does Jesus know you? Are you from Galilee, too, Simon? Why is he staying at your house?"

Why did Jesus sleep in Simon's house and eat at his table and fellowship with one whom everyone sought to avoid? I could understand if Jesus had stopped there. But Jesus lodged there; the Son of God, living with a broken-hearted, lonely leper! He was there because he is a loving Jesus and a saving Jesus. He said, "I was sick and you visited me. I was a stranger and you took me in. Inasmuch as you did to the least of these my brethren, you did it to me." This is the bottom line.

God Calls Us to Be Eagles

William D. Watley

Isaiah 40:27-31

The words of our text are words of encouragement to a people who were preparing to take upon themselves the arduous task of nation building. In the view of the prophet Isaiah, because of Israel's apostasy, the Lord had allowed Israel to be enslaved again—this time by the Babylonians. However, freedom had been secured when the Persian general Cyrus defeated the Babylonians and extended to the children of Israel, now the children of the Exile, the opportunity to return to their homeland. As the prophet had interpreted Israel's defeat within the perspective of God's providence, so he also recognized the hand of the Lord at work in those events that had led to Israel's liberation. Consequently, the prophet was given a new message to address Israel's new circumstances. Instead of upbraiding the people of Israel for their sins, his theme became one of comfort and encouragement. He said, "Comfort ye, comfort ye my people, saith your God. Speak ye comfortably to Jerusalem, and cry unto her, that her warfare is accomplished, that her iniquity is pardoned; for she hath received of the LORD's hand double for all her sins."

Whether one is rebuilding a life, a marriage, a church, a

race of people, a nation, or a school, reconstruction is never easy. Often there is opposition from forces without as well as dissension, confusion, and fear from within. The prophet knew all of this. That is the reason that in his call to the people of Israel to reclaim the greatness that had once been theirs and could still be their destiny, he reminded them of the omnipresent and omnipotent God who was on their side. He wrote, "Why do you cry, O Jacob, and speak, O Israel, 'My way is hid from the Lord, and my right is disregarded by my God'? Have you not known? Have you not heard? The Lord is the everlasting God, the Creator of the ends of the earth. He does not faint or grow weary; his understanding is unsearchable. He gives power to the faint, and to him who has no might he increases strength. Even youths shall faint and be weary and young men shall fall exhausted, but they who wait for the Lord shall renew their strength; they shall mount up with wings like eagles; they shall run and not be weary; they shall walk and not faint."

The eagle is a familiar and popular figure in the Scriptures. Its regal presence; its reputation as the king of birds; its dwelling in high and lofty places; its freedom, strength, and speed as epitomized in its majestic flight made the eagle in the minds of the biblical writers an appropriately fitting symbol for God in particular and for greatness in general. The eagle is also an appropriate symbol for that latent greatness inherent in all of those beings created by God to be human.

Although classified as fowl, eagles are not as easily produced as chickens and other birds. Eagles are not hatched in a brood. Nor is the reproductive cycle an overnight process. Chickens may be produced in twenty-one days and may be ready for the market in eight or nine weeks. But it takes time to produce an eagle. Eagles lay only one or two eggs, which are incubated by both parents for a relatively long period of time—up to forty-nine days in larger species. The young remain in the nest as long as one hundred thirty days before becoming fledglings and are fed by both parents. Among larger species of eagles the entire reproductive cycle may last more than twelve months so that successful breeding may take place only once every other year.

When I read the biblical account of the creation in Genesis, I am struck by the fact that God took the time to make a human being. God may have spoken forth the sun, the moon, and the stars; God may have decreed that the firmament come into being; God may have declared that fishes swim the ocean, that mammals roam the land, and that the birds split the air with their wings; but humans were not proclaimed into being. God took the time to make men and women. According to the anthropomorphic poetic musing of James Weldon Johnson:

> Then God sat down—
> On the side of a hill where he could think;
> By a deep, wide river he sat down;
> With his head in his hands,
> God thought and thought,
> Till he thought: I'll make me a man!
>
> Up from the bed of the river
> God scooped the clay;
> And by the bank of the river
> He kneeled him down;
> And there the great God Almighty
> Who lit the sun and fixed it in the sky,
> Who flung the stars to the most far corner of the night;
> Who rounded the earth in the middle of his hand;
> This Great God,
> Like a mammy bending over her baby,
> Kneeled down in the dust
> Toiling over a lump of clay
> Till he shaped it in his own image;
>
> Then into it he blew the breath of life,
> And man became. . . .

[Not just a moving, feeling thing, not just another creature, but man became]

                                                   . . . a living soul.[1]

It takes time to produce greatness. Babies are born every minute of every hour of every day, but Booker T. Washingtons and Marian Andersons, Albert Einsteins and Albert Schweitzers, Elizabeth Brownings and Madame Curies, Mahatma Gandhis and Kwame Nkrumahs are produced once every so often. It takes time and special effort and care to produce greatness.

The eagle is also a solitary bird. It dares to fly alone. Eagles never fly in flocks; only one or at most two are ever seen at

[1]James Weldon Johnson, *"Creation," God's Trombones* (New York: The Viking Press, 1927, 1955), pp. 19-20. Copyright renewed 1955 by Grace Nail Johnson. Reprinted by permission of Viking Penguin Inc.

once. God seeks eagle men and eagle women—persons who are not afraid to stand, walk, run, or fly alone; persons who are willing to walk with God even if it means being misunderstood or laughed at because of the causes that they believe in or the stand that they have taken because deep within their hearts they know that they are right; persons who dare to dream dreams and see visions of things that can be instead of nightmares of things that cannot be or cannot happen simply because "we've never done it before" or "we've not done it like this before" or "we tried it once long ago and it didn't work"; persons who love and trust God enough to follow wherever and however and whenever he directs them.

Although no person is an island sufficient unto himself or herself and although we are called to community, no person ever comes into full and complete relationship with God who does not learn to walk alone with God. It was when he was alone with God that Jacob became a prince. Moses was by himself when God called to him out of a burning bush. "The greatest miracles of Elijah and Elisha took place when they were alone with God. . . . Gideon and Jephthah were by themselves when commissioned to save Israel. . . . John the Baptist was alone in the wilderness. . . ."[2] Cornelius was by himself when the angel came to him. Peter was by himself on the housetop when he was instructed to go to the Gentiles. "Paul, who was filled with Greek learning and had also sat at the feet of the great rabbinical scholar Gamaliel, must go in to Arabia and learn the desert life with God."[3] John the Revelator was alone on Patmos when the risen, exalted, and reigning Christ pulled back the curtains of heaven and showed him visions of things that were yet to be.

Isaiah said one day, "I have trod the winepress alone." There will be times in our lives when we know that for the sake of those things that we really believe, we must be prepared, like the eagle, to fly alone. Being an eagle-person can be a lonely experience, not because all of us don't have the potential for greatness, but because it's easier and safer to spend our lives with the petty, the mundane, the mediocre, and the superficial and because most people follow the path that is easiest and

[2]Mrs. Charles E. Cowman, comp., *Streams in the Desert* (Grand Rapids: The Zondervan Corp., 1965), p. 65.
[3]*Ibid.*

offers the least resistance. Being an eagle-person can be a lonely experience because not everybody understands eagle-people. And what we don't understand, we fear, and what we fear, we either attack or malign or attempt to destroy.

Flying alone can be frightening when we realize our own limitations and how weak we really are and that we are hanging out there by ourselves while a multitude watches and waits for us to fall. But in those times we will discover that God will take care of us in the same way that a mother eagle looks after a young fledgling who is trying to learn to fly.

One day the mother eagle nudges her fledgling over the rim of the nest, high up on some rocky ledge. Suddenly the young bird finds itself hurtling through space and begins to beat its wings frantically in a desperate life-and-death struggle for survival. For a few moments it soars, but then its strength fails and it looks as if it will plunge to certain death. But the ever-present and watchful mother eagle swoops down beneath it and brings swift rescue and strong support on the pinions of her wings.

In the same way God looked after Israel. One writer said, "As an eagle stirreth up her nest, fluttereth over her young, spreadeth abroad her wings, taketh them, beareth them on her wings: So the LORD alone did lead him. . . ." In the same way the Lord takes care of us. I know that sometimes it appears that we are stretched out by ourselves; however, no one who flies leaning and depending on God ever flies by oneself, for "the eternal God is thy refuge, and underneath are the everlasting arms. . . ." And, as our text reminds us, "They that wait upon the LORD shall renew their strength; they shall mount up with wings as eagles; they shall run, and not be weary; and they shall walk, and not faint."

Eagles are known for the strength of their wings. The golden eagle, known as the king of birds, is powerful and majestic in its flight. With a wingspan of almost nine feet and weighing about fifteen pounds, it can fly effortlessly at sixty miles an hour. When it sights its prey, it can plunge at one hundred miles an hour, and with incredible strength it can swoop and lift an animal twice its own weight with ease. Eagles' wings are wings of power. With them eagles can glide through many storms.

According to E. Stanley Jones's account,

One day in India an eagle soared overhead, taking advantage of the rising air currents from the warm earth below. Then a strong wind began to blow, the sky grew dark, and in the distance a threatening storm cloud began to make its way across the land. At first the eagle flew away from the storm, as though in fear of it. Suddenly the eagle turned and drove directly toward the storm. Then, arching its wings against the force of the onrushing wind, he was vaulted upward, higher and higher, until at last he could be seen soaring in the calm air above the storm.[4]

To be an eagle-person is to be a person of power who, like the eagle, knows how to face the storms of life and rise above them. For storm clouds arise in all of our lives, and we had better mind how we react to and treat others when it's storming in their lives because, before we realize it, it can be storming in our lives. We can't run from storms; we must confront them in the strength of the Lord. We can stand and withstand even though we're being hit, buffetted, and beat upon from all sides. God hasn't given us the wings of a dove to fly away and be at rest. He has given us the wings of an eagle so that we can mount in the midst of the storm and declare, "I know in whom I have believed."

God has called us to be eagles. Therefore, be an eagle. Don't settle for anything less. For there are some who, because of meanness, jealousy, or their own lack of vision, will try to make a chicken out of you.

An old story has been passed down from one generation to another through the black preaching tradition. It's about a man who was hiking in the hills near his home one day and found a strange-looking egg. This man happened to own a poultry farm; so he placed this strange-looking egg in the incubator to be hatched with the other eggs. In time, this strange-looking egg produced a strange-looking bird. And so it was that even though it had a peculiar air about it and was obviously out of place among the other birds, the farmer decided that he would raise the bird like a chicken since chickens were all he had ever raised. Soon, because all this bird ever saw were chickens, because all he was ever given to eat was chicken feed, because day in and day out he was treated like a chicken, because the only name he was ever called was "chicken," this

[4]Charles L. Wallis, ed., *The Ministers Manual (Doran's)*, 1981 ed. (San Francisco: Harper & Row, Publishers, Inc., 1980), p. 250.

bird began to act like a chicken. He lost his peculiar air and no longer seemed so out of place.

One day a visitor came to the farm, and while he was walking through the yard, he saw this strange-looking bird. He walked up to the farmer and asked him why he had an eagle living among his chickens.

The farmer replied, "He may look like an eagle, but I have raised him to be a chicken. He lives among chickens; he eats like a chicken; the only life he knows is the life of a chicken. So a chicken is all he will ever be."

The visitor said, "You cannot callously tamper with the soul of God's creation. God has placed within this bird the seeds for greatness, and you have confined it to the barnyard. However, no creature that God has intended for flying in lofty places is beyond redemption, no matter how long it has been in the barnyard. This bird may have the habits of a chicken, but deep down within, where your environment can't reach, God has placed the heart and soul of an eagle."

The visitor lifted the eagle and said, "God did not create you to be a chicken. God created you to be an eagle; so stretch forth your wings and fly." The eagle took off from the visitor's hand. But as it was ascending, the farmer threw some chicken feed on the ground, and the eagle flew right back to the ground and started eating the feed. The farmer looked at the visitor and said: "I told you that he was nothing but a chicken."

At this point, the visitor took the eagle and climbed to the top of the barn where the eagle could see a little more of the countryside and behold that there was a world beyond the barnyard. He told the eagle a second time, "God did not create you to be a chicken but an eagle; so stretch forth your wings and fly."

Again the bird took off, ascending. Again the farmer threw feed to the ground, and again the eagle flew down to the ground. The farmer once more turned to the visitor and said, "I told you that he was nothing but a chicken."

Refusing to give up, the visitor asked the farmer if he could try one more time. Early the next morning, while it was yet dark, the visitor placed the eagle under his arm and started climbing up a high mountain. As he approached the summit, the sun was beginning to break the darkness of the eastern horizon. The visitor pointed the eagle toward the rising sun and said a third time, "You were not created to be a chicken but an eagle, so stretch your wings and fly." The rays of the rising sun struck the piercing gleam in the eagle's eye; his body began to tremble with pulsating energy, and with one great leap, on outstretched wings, the eagle flew away toward the dawning of the new day—not looking back and not looking down—only toward the greatness that God intended.

One day when the evil one held our souls in captivity and we were subjected to a barnyard existence, a visitor from glory, who was the creative and redemptive Word made flesh, came to dwell with us for a season. He told us that we didn't have to live in the barnyard of sin and slavery, that God had created us to live eternally with him in high and lofty places. One Friday he bore a cross up a hill called Calvary and early that Sunday, while it was yet dark, he set our souls eternally free. The announcement was made, "He is not here; he is risen!"

Now when this society tells us that since God has blessed us with an ebony complexion, all we can be is chickens, we can face a frowning world and declare, "Beloved, we are God's children now. It does not yet appear what we shall be, but we know that when he appears we shall be like him, for we shall see him as he is."

Now when oppressive whites and narrow-minded blacks try to take away our eagle-ness, we can tell them, "He whom the Son sets free is free indeed."

Giants Keep Coming[1]

William D. Watley

2 Samuel 21:15-22

Most of us are familiar with the story of David and the giant Goliath. At a time when Saul was king of Israel and David was only a shepherd boy, the Israelites and the Philistines were once again at war. As the two armies lined up and squared off to face each other on the battlefield, a Philistine warrior named Goliath issued a challenge to the armies of Israel. He told the Israelites, "We don't need a whole army to settle the dispute between our two nations. I will represent the Philistines. You pick from among yourselves someone to represent Israel, and we two will battle. If he defeats me, then we will be your slaves, and if I defeat him, then you will be our slaves."

Goliath's challenge totally demoralized the armies of Israel, for Goliath not only talked big—Goliath was big. Standing over nine feet tall, he wore a coat of mail weighing two hundred pounds and carried a javelin for a spear, which had an iron spearhead that weighed twenty-five pounds. For some forty days Goliath strutted back and forth in front of the armies of

[1]The integrity of the craft mandates that I recognize my colleague, Dr. John Bryant, pastor of Bethel A.M.E. Church, of Baltimore, Maryland, for providing the human inspiration for this message.

Israel issuing his challenge and insulting them. And for some forty days King Saul searched in vain among his troops for someone with either the courage, faith, tenacity, or reckless abandon to take on a giant.

In the meantime Jesse grew concerned about three of his sons who were in Saul's army. So Jesse called his youngest son, David, from the field and sent him to his brethren on the battlefield to take some food and to inquire about their well-being.

When David arrived on the scene of battle, the situation looked pretty bleak for Israel. No one seemed to know what to do, and the dark circles under King Saul's eyes and his worried and harried gaze reflected the state of a man who carried the weight of the nation upon his shoulders. He had spent many sleepless nights trying to figure a way out of his dilemma while his generals remained divided among themselves and confused with respect to strategy. They, like Saul, did not know what to do. Let it be observed that whenever leadership speaks with a hesitating and frightened voice, whenever leadership appears to be confused and groping, whenever there is division at the top, those attitudes have a way of filtering down and affecting the spirits and attitudes of the rank and file. And so it was that a sense of hopelessness had gripped and paralyzed the minds, the spirits, and the hearts of Saul's soldiers.

When David saw the plight of Israel, coupled with the brashness and arrogance of Goliath, he stepped forth to challenge the giant. Naturally when he did so, people looked at him in disbelief. The king told him, "You're just a boy and the giant that you propose to fight is not only fully grown but has been fighting since he was a boy."

But David said, "The same God who allows me to defeat the bears and the lions who attack my sheep and who is my rod and staff and who comforts me is able to give me the victory over this Philistine." And so David, using the same weapons that had brought him thus far—his slingshot and his faith—went forth to meet Goliath. The outcome we all know. David, the young shepherd boy, defeated Goliath, the seasoned, giant Philistine warrior.

Traditionally, without giving much thought to the matter, a number of us have concluded that the story of his battle with Goliath comprises the sum total of David's experience and of his dealings with giants. However, according to our text, years later—when David himself had become a seasoned warrior and an old man; when David, who was once Saul's armor bearer and valet, had become Saul's successor to the throne of Israel; when David, the shepherd boy, had become King David, monarch of Israel, and had reigned for many years—David had to fight some other giants.

The Scriptures tell us that years later, after the battle with the Philistine giant Goliath, Israel and the Philistines were again at war, and a giant named Ishbibenob, whose spear tip weighed over twelve pounds and who sported a new suit of armor, sought to kill David. But Abishai, one of David's troops, came to the rescue. At that point David's men began to express some concern for his well-being, telling him, "You shall no more go to battle with us, lest you be killed and the light of Israel be quenched."

After this, David's troops fought the Philistines again; Elhanan, another of David's troops, slew the brother of Goliath the Gittite, who was a giant and whose spear was the size of a weaver's beam. Still later at another place and time during David's reign, his troops faced another giant who was so great in stature that he had six fingers on each hand and six toes on each foot. Jonathan, the son of David's brother Shimeah, slew him. And during still another war with the Philistines, Sibbechai, one of David's men, killed Saph, another giant. All of these giants fought on the side of the Philistines against David and his troops, and they were all defeated. You see, with David the giants just kept coming.

It makes no difference who you are or how great or vicious or powerful your own personal Goliath may have been or how impressive your victory over him, her, or it may have been, nobody, but nobody, goes through life with only one giant to face. You ought never to allow yourself to be fooled into believing that Satan, your Philistine adversary, who still roves to and fro like a wounded, raging, and hungry lion seeking whom he may devour, has only one giant for you to face. Sooner or later, we all, like David, discover that in this life giants keep coming.

True, there may be some giants who stand out as major hurdles, major obstacles, and major hindrances, and our claim to fame may be partially based on victories over certain major trials, problems, or handicaps. During our lives, however, there will be other battles in which we will meet other giants. These other battles may not be as famous as David and Goliath's, and these other giants may not be as famous as Goliath of Gath. Others may not discuss them as much, and many persons may not even be aware of these other battles and these other giants. But whether known to others or not, they still must be dealt with because each giant has within himself the potential and the wherewithal to defeat us. Let us never forget that all giants must be taken seriously because the goal of each giant is our destruction.

As black Americans we know what it is for giants to keep coming. For over three hundred years we fought the giant of slavery. Then for another one hundred years we fought the giant of Jim Crow. In the 1960s we fought the giants of Southern hostility. In the 1970s we fought the giants of Northern backlash on the one hand and benign neglect on the other. In the 1980s we are fighting the giant of national apathy. We've had to fight the giants of slavery, racial discrimination, economic poverty, an educational system that is separate and unequal, demeaning self-images, psychological put-downs, systemic violence, unjust systems of justice. For us the giants keep coming.

We've fought giants from without, not only on a social level but also on a personal level. Sometimes those giants are other people whose only goal in life seems to be to make us miserable. Life would be so much more pleasant without some people always there to pick at us. Sometimes giants from without come in the form of circumstances—sickness, accidents, misfortune, setbacks and disappointments, trials and problems. Whenever we get one problem solved, another crops up to take its place. We get one problem worked out in our home or with our marriage, and before we can recover, another difficulty appears. We handle one situation on our jobs, and we are hit with another while we are still shaking from the first shock. We handle one crisis in our church, and we are hit with another. It just seems that when we have mastered one giant, up pops another to take its place. The giants just keep coming.

All of our giants, however, are not from without; some of the greatest and most deadly giants that we will have to face come from within. Many are the persons who have been victorious over the giants without but have lost the battle to the giants within. "For what shall it profit a man, if he shall gain the whole world, and lose his own soul?" Many an individual has been victorious over outward circumstances, but the strain of the battle has left the spirit embittered and broken, with the zest for living gone from the heart. Some people have fought so many giants for so long that the battles have left them shell-shocked and battle weary—no song in their souls, no joy in their religion, no hope in their view.

You're going to discover that some of your biggest battles will not be in public view where sympathetic onlookers can offer encouragement and comfort. They will be in your secret chamber, where nobody but you and the Lord will know about how hard you have had to struggle and with what you have had to struggle just to keep on keeping on. Sometimes your greatest giants will be fought not by standing on your feet but by falling on your knees and asking God to keep your heart from bitterness and your spirit from vindictiveness when you think about some of the mean things that people have said about you or done to you.

It's interesting to me that David faced Goliath when he was a young boy and that he faced the other giants when he was an old man. David faced his giants during those periods of his life when many would conclude that he was either too young or too old to contend with giants. He faced his giants when he was least prepared to do battle with them.

Giants not only keep coming, but they come upon us also when we are least able to resist them. They are respecters of neither age nor conditions, and so they come when we are at our weakest and most unprepared to battle them. Don't expect always to fight giants when you are at your strongest. Expect to fight them in weakness. It was not immediately after Jesus had been baptized by John in the Jordan River and the Spirit had been poured afresh upon him that Satan appeared. No, it was after Jesus had been in the wilderness for forty days without food that Satan appeared to him and said, "You don't have to take all of this. You don't have to go through all of this. If you are really the Son of God, command that these stones be turned to bread."

I realize that contending with giants in our weakness can be frightening, but let us not forget that when David became too old and too weak to fight, he had some troops to help him fight his battles. Jesus knew that the giants of "principalities and powers," the giants who "rule this present darkness," the giants of "spiritual wickedness in high places" were too powerful for us to resist by ourselves. That's why he told the disciples, "I'm going to send you a comforter, the Holy Spirit, that shall lead you into all truth, and you shall receive power after the Holy Ghost is come upon you, and you shall be my witnesses in Jerusalem, in all Judaea, in Samaria, and in the uttermost parts of the earth."

I am so glad that the God who made us knows how weak we are. He knows that there are some giants that we cannot defeat by ourselves. Like David, sinful humanity discovered a giant that was more fierce than the rest. That was a giant called death. Men and women had been able to conquer every other giant except the giant of death. Abraham, the father of the faithful, couldn't do it, and Moses, the great lawgiver, couldn't do it. Joshua and Gideon, generals of the armies of God's covenant people, couldn't do it. Samuel, Isaiah, and the other prophets couldn't do it. Job with his patience couldn't do it, and Amos with his zeal for social justice couldn't do it. Daniel with his courage couldn't do it, and Hosea with his all-forgiving love couldn't do it. Solomon with his wisdom couldn't do it. David was God's king and the man after God's own heart, but even he couldn't do it. John the Baptist, the wayfaring voice crying in the wilderness, couldn't conquer old death.

So God, in the wisdom of divine providence, sent the supreme giant slayer whose name was Jesus who, after having wrapped himself up in the garments of human flesh, stepped down through forty-two generations and dwelt among us. He did good and was crucified. When he died, death told the grave, "He was a good man, but we have him along with all the others. His body is ours to claim, and his spirit is ours to keep." But early that Sunday morning, Jesus Christ, the Lamb of God, the Rose of Sharon, the Prince of Peace, snatched the sting from death, took the victory from the grave, led captivity captive, and rose to stoop no more.

Giants may keep coming, but with Jesus on our side, the

bigger they come, the harder they fall. Let giants come because we have this word of assurance from Christ:

> "While thus ye follow my commands,
> I'm with you till the world shall end,
> All power is trusted in my hands,
> I can destroy, and can defend."[2]

[2]"Go Preach My Gospel."

Standing on Clay Feet

William D. Watley

Daniel 2:31-35

Chapter 2 of Daniel tells of an intriguing incident that occurred in the life and reign of Nebuchadnezzar, king of Babylon. One night Nebuchadnezzar had a strange dream. The next morning when he awakened, he was frightened and possessed with an eerie feeling. He had a sense of foreboding and dread that he could not shake. He knew that there was an important message in that dream for him, and he was beside himself, for not only did he not know what that message was but he also couldn't even remember the dream.

So he called all of his wise men, astrologers, root workers, tea-leaf and palm readers, and hoodoo people together and demanded that they tell him what his dream was and what it meant. Naturally they could not. They told him that if he could remember his dream, they could interpret it, but they were powerless to know what he had dreamed, and it was unreasonable of him to expect them to know.

Nebuchadnezzer was so vexed in spirit and disturbed in mind that he ordered all of the wise men in the land to be killed since they couldn't tell him his dream. It's terrible to be in such agony of soul, turmoil of spirit, and confusion of mind that we lash out in panic and fury, without forethought of the consequences or of the possible injury to the innocent.

As the soldiers were rounding up the wise men of the land, they encountered a Jewish prophet whose name was Daniel. When Daniel inquired as to what was happening and was told, he did what he was accustomed to doing at least three times every day. He went to his God in prayer and asked that the dream, along with the interpretation, might be revealed to him. And his God, who was only a prayer away, heard Daniel's pleadings and gave to him those things for which he asked.

So Daniel went before Nebuchadnezzar and said, "I have the answers that you're looking for. I have them, not because I'm smarter than everybody else. I just happen to know a God to whom all desires are known and from whom no secrets are hid, for whom the darkest mystery is as clear as the noonday sun on a bright summer's day, who will reveal to his children the deep secrets of life. There are some answers that you can't find in a root or a tea cup or in the palm of your hand. There are some questions that only God can answer. There are some things that only the Spirit of the Lord can reveal and make known to you as you seek him in earnest prayer.

"This God to whom I belong and whom I serve has revealed to me your dream. You saw a huge and powerful image of a man. It shone brilliantly and was frightening to behold. Its head was made of gold; its chest and arms were of silver. Its abdomen and thighs were made of bronze; its legs were made of iron, and its feet were partly of iron and partly of clay."

This image had to be a mighty powerful, a mighty heavy, and a mighty awesome statue because it was made of some of the most valuable and most durable metals in the world. It was made of gold and silver, which are kept for their monetary value. It was made of bronze, which is valued for its durability, and of iron, which is valued for its strength. It had only one problem—it had bad, weak feet. The value and strength of the rest of the statue was supported by a foundation of clay. The whole body, with all of its brilliance, awesomeness, and terrifying demeanor, stood, nevertheless, on clay feet.

This nation of ours presents a powerful image to the rest of the world of what human ingenuity can build. We have a head of pure gold. Our standard of living is higher than any other in the world. As inconceivable as it may be to us, there are countries where the average income for persons like you and me is fifty dollars a *year*. While we're paying farmers not to grow food, while we use our grain as a means for gaining political leverage, while leftovers sour in our refrigerators, the vast majority of the world's population goes to bed hungry every night. As poor as we as black Americans are when compared to the majority of whites, we are still the best fed, best dressed, best housed oppressed people in the world. We wear the best clothes, drink the best scotch, and drive some of the most expensive cars. We as Americans are an arrogant, spoiled, selfish people with heads of gold.

Not only do we have a golden head, but we have a chest and arms of silver. Next to money, our knowledge is the most valuable thing to us. We have used our knowledge to help us make more money, to help support our head of gold. We have used our knowledge to build huge skyscrapers, symbols of our opulent life-style, whose spires pierce the skies and tickle the passing clouds. We have used our knowledge to build sophisticated weapons systems that can wipe out whole populations in the twinkling of an eye. Our computers and technology have become the new shepherds by which we expect to be led to even greener pastures. With our silvery arms of knowledge we have reached out into countries where we have no business and have exploited them and have attempted to run and ruin the lives of their people. We have used our knowledge not to uplift humanity but all too often to exploit, oppress, and suppress humanity.

The image that appears before the world not only has a wealthy head of gold with an educated chest and arms of silver that know how, when, and where to reach, but also has a bronze religious abdomen and thighs. As we use our knowledge to justify our sins logically, so we use our religion to justify our sins morally. We think the purpose of religion is to comfort us and to make us feel good. Religion may comfort us when we need comforting, but it is not just about comfort. It is also about something called righteousness, and it condemns something called sin. Religion not only supports us when we're right but also condemns us when we are wrong. It not only makes us feel good, but when we sin, it also makes us feel bad by reminding us that no matter what excuses we give, no matter how many big words we use to justify ourselves or make our actions appear alright, sin is still sin. And even if everybody is doing it, God's Word says: "Be not deceived; God is not mocked: for whatsoever a man soweth, that shall he also reap," and ". . . the wages of sin is death; but the gift of God is eternal life through Jesus Christ our Lord."

We have used our religion to legitimate our exploitation and oppression of others. As we are aware, the only reason that whites taught Christianity to blacks was that they thought it would make us better slaves. They twisted the gospel message to teach us that God created us inferior and foreordained that we be nothing but hewers of wood and drawers of water. But someway, somehow, God through the Holy Spirit saw to it that enough truth seeped through so that, in spite of what we were told, we received the message: we are God's children, created in his own image and made by his very own hand, and even if we wore chains, we know that one day on Calvary Jesus set us free and "he whom the Son sets free is free indeed." From the drippings of a watered-down distorted gospel that fell from the lips of white racists we were able to extrapolate some golden nuggets of truth about the freedom and salvation that God really wills for his children. We didn't have formal education, but God gave us common, or should I say uncommon, sense enough to know a lie from the truth.

The story is told of a Southern church during the time of antebellum slavery. In many churches blacks were confined to the balconies called "galleys," which were also euphemistically referred to as "nigger heavens." One Sunday morning, as the story goes, a white preacher was exhorting the slaves and told them, "When you darkies get to heaven, it will be the same way up there as it is down here. We whites will sit on the main floor, and you will be in the galleys."

This disturbed the slaves; so that night they decided to meet by the bush arbor to discuss it. The indigenous preacher stood up and told the slaves, "Did you hear what that preacher told us this morning? He told us that in heaven the whites would sit on the main floor and we would be in the galleys. I'll tell you what 'us' ought to do. Let's all get to heaven early, and let's all take the main seats on the main floor; and then when they get there, if they don't want to sit there with us, let them go to hell."

You can't use religion to justify wrong; someway God will

see to it that truth and right be seen, no matter how much we try to hide them or pervert them.

Not only does this American image have a wealthy head of gold, a silvery chest and arms of knowledge, a bronze abdomen and thighs of religion, but it also has iron legs of militarism. We are still trying to police the whole world. For years we told ourselves and others that we were protecting the world and making it safe for democracy. But Vietnam showed us to be the liars that we are. A nation doesn't protect anybody by dropping napalm on them or bombing their villages or killing their children. A nation doesn't make the world safe for democracy by helping to undermine revolutions in South America and Africa where people are trying to get what we claim we're trying to give them—freedom—or by supporting dictatorships in the Philippines and apartheid in South Africa. We're not boss because we're right but because we're big and bad enough to be boss. We have yet to learn the lesson from the prophet, "Not by might, nor by power, but by my spirit saith the LORD of hosts."

This image called America, no matter how terrifying or invincible it may appear to be, is in trouble, for the whole thing is standing on clay feet. When we read Max Weber's work *The Protestant Ethic and the Spirit of Capitalism*, we see that he expounds the thesis that the reason this country is so great is that the Puritans combined the virtues of hard work, honesty, and thrift to make this country what it is today. But some of us know that while this country claims to stand on the Puritan ethic of hard work, honesty, and thrift, it actually is built upon the sweat, blood, labor, and tears of black slaves. Whites accumulated such huge fortunes because they had free slave labor.

W.E.B. Dubois, in *The Gift of Black Folk*, points out that the gift of labor is "one of the greatest that the Negro has made to American nationality. It was in part involuntary, but whether given willingly or not, it *was* given, and America profited from the gift." You see, it was our labor that helped to build the cities of the North and we helped make cotton king in the South. We prepared the food of the nation. We built schools for other people's children to attend and cleared the forests and frontiers for the railroad. When the nation went to war, we spilled our blood alongside others.

Whenever we as a nation build ourselves up by taking advantage of either the innocence or trust or the misfortunes or sufferings of others, then we're standing on clay feet. Whenever we build ourselves up by manipulating, misusing, or abusing any of God's children, then we're standing on clay feet, and as sure as we're born to die, the judgment of the Lord is upon us. Whenever we don't care who we use or how we use them or who we step on to get where we want to go, then we're standing on clay feet. Whenever we take from others and give back little or nothing in return, whether we are a nation, a corporation, or an individual or a church, then we're standing on clay feet. Whenever we forget that God has said, "Let not the wise man glory in his wisdom, neither let the mighty man glory in his might, let not the rich man glory in his riches. But let him who glories glory in this, that he understands and knows me, that I am the Lord who practices steadfast love, justice, and righteousness in the earth; for in these things I delight," then we're standing on clay feet.

If there is any lesson to learn from Nebuchadnezzar's dream, it is that images that stand on clay feet, no matter how great they are, do not stand forever. Daniel tells us that from out of nowhere a stone, a rock cut without hands, rolled down from a mountain and fell on the feet of the image, making the whole statue collapse and break into pieces. I believe that moving through the events of history is an unseen hand that is weaving the separate, disparate, and disjointed strands of history into a perfect whole. Some people call it "the hand of fate," while others refer to it as "destiny." Some call it "providence," and still others call it "determinism" and "predestination." I know whose hand it is; it is the hand of God. And every now and then—from out of nowhere—God causes things to happen in order to let us know that he still lives and he still rules and superrules over his creation and he is not pleased with the things we have done.

And so it was one day, when the world and America were looking at the image America had made of itself, that from out of nowhere a black woman, whose ancestors had been part of the feet that the whole American image had been standing on, a black woman by the name of Rosa Parks, who was an A.M.E. stewardess, boarded a bus in Montgomery, Alabama. When asked to get up and give her seat to a white male passenger, she decided—because her feet were tired, because she was tired of being "'buked and scorned," tired of supporting a huge military-industrial complex, tired of being the last hired and first fired, tired of a Jim Crow life-style, tired of being treated as if she had no rights that whites were duty bound to respect— that she wasn't going to move.

And it happened that God had arranged providence so that in the same place and at the same time he had placed, as pastor of a Baptist church in Montgomery, a young twenty-five-year-old Ph.D. from Boston University whose name was Martin Luther King, Jr. From out of nowhere, in Montgomery, Alabama, the capital of the Old Confederacy, King came forth proclaiming that "the arc of the moral universe may be long but it bends towards justice" and that "truth crushed to earth shall rise again."

When those blacks started proclaiming, "We'd rather walk in dignity than ride in shame," they set off a chain reaction all over the country. All over this nation blacks, young and old, educated and uneducated, found new courage to stop laughing when they weren't tickled, to stop scratching where they weren't itching, to stop marking time, and to start marching. When blacks started marching, so did Native Americans, Hispanics, women, and people devoted to international peace. This old image of Amercia began to reel and rock, and it hasn't stopped shaking yet. And only God knows whether it will stand or fall.

God moves from out of nowhere. The rock that shattered the image in Nebuchadnezzar's dream became a mountain that filled the whole earth. Some two thousand years ago from out of nowhere—from the foothills of Galilee in the backwoods town of Nazareth—a young thirty-year-old carpenter-turned-preacher came forth and established a kingdom in the hearts of believing men and women and girls and boys. That kingdom still stands.

If your kingdoms are built upon clay feet, I invite you to join a kingdom that's built upon a Rock, and that Rock is Jesus. Caesar's Rome fell, Napoleon's France fell, Mussolini's Italy fell, and Hitler's Germany fell. Stalin's Russia, Mao Tse-tung's China, and the Puritan's America may one day fall, but I know about a King and a kingdom that shall stand forever. "The grass withers, the flower fades, but the word of our God will stand forever."

This kingdom has to stand. You see, Caesar, Hitler, Napoleon, and the others have all gone for good, but the Jesus who started this kingdom is coming back again to judge the quick and the dead, to claim a church without spot or wrinkle, and to reward those whose names appear in the kingdom's *Who's Who*, better known as the Lamb's book of life. He told his disciples one day,

"Let not your heart be troubled; ye believe in God, believe also in me. In my Father's house are many mansions; if it were not so, I would have told you. I go to prepare a place for you. And if I go and prepare a place for you, I will come again, and receive you unto myself; that where I am, there ye may be also."

Good News from the Graveyard

William D. Watley

Matthew 28:5-7

Graveyards are not usually associated with joy and hope. If you are depressed and feeling bad, one of the least likely places in which you would consider finding relief and release is a graveyard. The great scientific discoveries that have done so much to revolutionize our daily living have been made in all kinds of places and under all kinds of circumstances. Nothing of scientific significance, however, has ever been discovered in a graveyard. The great battles of history have been fought in all kinds of places—on land and on sea, in the air and on the plains, on mountains and in valleys, in great cities and humble villages. However, no great battles have been fought in graveyards. With the possible exception of the Gettysburg Address, no great speeches or pronouncements from leading orators, ministers, poets, or rulers have ever been made in graveyards. If you ever want to see something of significance or hear something good, the last place that you would consider looking is a graveyard. Graveyards, after all, are for dead people, and as we all know, dead people do not move or speak. And if they ever did, most of us would not stay around long enough to see much of what they might do or hear much of what they might say.

Yet if Easter is about anything, it is about the Good News that comes out of a graveyard. Easter, one of the biggest and one of the most significant (if not the biggest and the most significant) observances of the Christian faith comes out of a borrowed tomb, of all places. Easter, with all of the joy and all of the hope that it brings, was set in a graveyard. It did not occur at the banks of the Jordan River with the heavens opening up and the Spirit of God descending like a dove and the voice of God thundering forth, but in, of all places, a lonely graveyard. It did not take place on the Mount of Transfiguration or in the busy streets of Jerusalem amidst the cheering crowds of Palm Sunday but in a lonely graveyard.

If Easter is about anything, it is the announcement and celebration of the Good News that love conquers hate, right conquers wrong, and nonviolence defeats violence. It is the message that good, though seemingly always on the run and on the ropes, can still conquer evil, and that holiness, without compromising itself or stooping to use the methods of the opponent, can still defeat sin. If the fact that all of this Good News comes out of a graveyard seems strange, let me remind you that Christianity is a strange faith. To begin with, its premise is the strange assertion that a God whose greatness and magnitude is beyond comprehension, is concerned about, cares for, and loves puny, insignificant human beings so much that to save us this God became one with us and one of us.

And if that sounds strange, listen to this! Christianity would have you believe not only that God became a man but also that God became a poor man—he was born in a stable to poor parents and an oppressed people in one of the smallest countries of the world. When he was born, angels sang not to the high priest and the religious leaders but to lowly shepherds.

And if that sounds strange, listen to this! Christianity would have you believe that this God, being born a man, associated with fishermen, tax collectors, prostitutes, and all kinds of what we would call "lower class, common people," and "sinners."

And if that sounds strange, listen to this! Christianity would have you believe that when Jesus, the God-man, rode into Jerusalem as a king, he rode not in a chariot but on a donkey and that he was greeted not with trumpets but with palms. His army consisted, not of trained soldiers, but of ordinary poor men and women, girls and boys. Whoever heard of a king riding a donkey, without armed soldiers, without royal robes, without blasting trumpets?

And if that sounds strange, listen to this! Christianity would have you believe that even though he could have called ten thousand angels to destroy the world and set him free, Jesus allowed himself to be beaten and bruised and judged in the kangaroo courts of ancient Palestine and then to be crucified between two thieves, like one of the worst of criminals.

And if that sounds strange, listen to this! This same Jesus, who opened blinded eyes and cut loose stammering tongues, who healed the sick and raised the dead, and who calmed raging seas claimed that it would be Calvary, with all of its pain and shame, that would glorify and exalt him. It was this same Jesus who said, "And I, if I be lifted up from the earth, will draw all men unto me." So then, when one considers how strange the Christian faith is anyway, it's not strange after all that the Good News it has for all of humankind comes from a graveyard.

Just what is this Good News that comes out of a graveyard? Well, the first thing that the angel at the tomb told the women was "Fear not." We have become very fearful these days. We lock ourselves in our homes behind four and five locks, wrought-iron gates, and barred windows. Not only are we prisoners in our homes but the fear of the violence of the streets holds our minds captive and keeps our spirits bound when we venture out. We are afraid of each other. We fear our spouses, our children, our parents, and other relatives. We are threatened by our employers, skeptical of our associates and colleagues, and afraid to trust our friends. We have forgotten that God's Word tells us to "Fear not!" God lives and God still watches over his own. If God is for us, who then can prevail against us? Therefore we need fear no power, force, or opposition; no sickness, circumstance or condition; no person (black or white, male or female); no angel or demon or principality; no height and no depth; nothing present and nothing to come. Fear not. We are more than conquerors through Christ Jesus who loves us. Fear not. "For he whom the Son sets free is free indeed." Fear not.

In ev'ry condition—in sickness, in health;
In poverty's vale, or abounding in wealth;

At home and abroad; on the land, on the sea,
"As thy days may demand, shall thy strength ever be."[1]

The second statement the angel made to the women was "He is not here; for he is risen." And that's certainly good news. Our Lord was lied about, but lies couldn't hold him down. He is risen! Our Lord was hated, but hate couldn't hold him down. He is risen! His opponents were jealous of him, but jealousy couldn't hold him down. He is risen! Jesus was persecuted, but persecution couldn't hold him down. He is risen! He was slandered, but slander couldn't hold him down. He is risen! In the end, he was killed, but not even death, the grave, and all the powers of hell and the forces of darkness could hold him down. He is risen!

Because he lives, truth lives, hope endures, love triumphs, and virtue is justified. Because he lives, integrity is legitimated, honesty has overcome, righteousness is proven, and sanctification is empowered. Because he lives, holiness is real, salvation has come, grace is all-sufficient, and mercy is invincible. Most of all, because he lives, we live also. "Therefore, if any one is in Christ, he is a new creation; the old has passed away; behold, all things have become new."

Then, third, the angel told the women, "Tell his disciples that he is risen and that he goeth before you into Galilee." That's why we can walk by faith rather than by sight. We know not only that our Lord walks with us but that he also goes before us. I don't know about you, but I am a witness that if you trust his promises, the Lord will go before you to straighten out situations before you get to them. He will go before you into a church meeting, and by the time you get there, he will have smoothed the ruffled waters. I know that it gets rough sometimes, but that same Jesus who sends you into the storm is also able to go before and smooth the rough, make straight the crooked, exalt the valleys, and level off the mountains.

You say that nothing of significance ever happened in a graveyard? I say unto you that humankind's greatest discovery occurred not when the atom was split or when we learned to harness and channel the power of electricity. Neither did it take place in a school or laboratory. Our greatest discovery occurred when a few women went to a graveyard looking to

[1]"How Firm a Foundation."

anoint the dead body of a good man and discovered a living Lord with a glorified body and with the keys to hell and death and life and eternity in his hands. The greatest battle that humankind ever fought was not at Waterloo, Gettysburg, or Hiroshima. Our greatest battle was fought in a lonely graveyard when Jesus Christ took on death, hell, and the demonic.

The Good News that I have come to announce to you is that *Jesus won!* He is the victor now, the winner henceforth, and the champion forevermore. He is King of kings, and he is Lord of lords. The greatest pronouncement that was ever made to humankind did not originate at the United Nations or in the Oval Office at the White House. It came, rather, from a graveyard when the angel of the Lord spoke to several women and said, "Fear not ye; for I know that ye seek Jesus who was crucified. He is not here; for he has risen, as he said. Come, see the place where the Lord lay. Then go quickly and tell his disciples that he has risen from the dead, and behold, he is going before you into Galilee; there you will see him."

So then it was not only in the deed of the cross but also in all that came out of a graveyard that first Easter morning that shows once again that "God hath chosen the foolish things of the world to confound the wise; and God hath chosen the weak things of the world to confound the things which are mighty; and base things of the world, and the things which are despised, hath God chosen, yea, and things which are not, to bring to nought things that are."

And so from a lonely graveyard comes a message that still gladdens the hearts of people everywhere who hear it—He lives! He lives! Glory, hallelujah! He lives!

73926

252.06/ LINCOLN CHRISTIAN COLLEGE
P964